PRAISE F

In The
Artists Speak

"This guy! I plead the fifth. This guy is nuts."

- Eminem

"Dope questions, man. Very insightful, very thoughtful."

- Guru (GangStarr)

"You like a Psychiatrist or some shit? This shit is just coming out but go ahead."

- Mary J. Blige

"Definitely a real interview! Digging deep up in there, man. Not afraid to ask questions!"

- K-Ci Hailey (Jodeci)

"The Wizard asked me for a copy of your magazine."

- Guy-Manuel de Homem-Christo (Daft Punk)

"You didn't wear your glasses and you haven't carried your hearing aid. What else is wrong with you?"

- Bushwick Bill

"Peace and blessing, Brother Harris. Thank you for inspiring my words. Keep 'yo balance."

- Erykah Badu

"Can I see that pen?"

- Bobby Brown

"What else do you want to know? Talk to me."

- Aaliyah

FREE BOOKS:

My archives are deep!

There are hundreds of interviews and dozens of books to follow.

That's why I am giving you a copy of New York State of Mind (Part 1) for free.

To receive your free copy of New York State of Mind (Part 1) and vintage exclusive 1992 and 1993 interviews with Intelligent Hoodlum/Tragedy Khadafi, Pete Rock & C.L. Smooth, Leaders of the New School and Brand Nubian – Soldiers sign up to our mailing list with your first name and email at behindthemusictales.com

The In Their Own Words: Behind the Music Tales of Truth, Fiction & Desire series has allowed me to share my extensive archive of exclusive interviews with you in much greater depth.

Some of the upcoming series you will hear exclusive audio and see exclusive photos are:

The Real Eminem: Broke City Trash Rapper

Daft Punk: Behind the Robots

Destiny's Child: The Writing's On The Wall

Beyonce, Kim, LeToya and LaTavia

New York State of Mind (Part 1)

Intelligent Hoodlum, Brand Nubian, Pete Rock & C.L. Smooth, Leaders of the New School

New York State of Mind (Part 2)

Afrika Bambaataa, Sean Combs, DMX, Funkmaster Flex

Magnolia: Home of tha Soldiers

Behind the Scenes with the Hot Boys & Cash Money Millionaires

Lil Wayne, Juvenile, B.G., Turk, Mannie Fresh, Birdman and Godfather Slim

pr-EDM (Part 1)

Kevin Saunderson, Moby, Malcolm McLaren and Todd Terry

The Grunge Years: 1989 - 1991

Nirvana, Pearl Jam, Alice In Chains, Soundgarden and Courtney Love

Legends of Hip-Hop (Part 1)

RUN-DMC, Beastie Boys, GangStarr and Nas

Ice-T, Bodycount & the Home Invasion of America

The Evolution of Funk, Rhythm & Soul (Part 1)

George Clinton, Bobby Brown, TLC and Erykah Badu

Deep Inside the Real Mary J. Blige

The Metal Years

Metallica, Megadeth, Slayer, Exodus, Iron Maiden, White Zombie

Rock N' Roll Legends (Part 1)

Kiss, The Replacements, The Black Crowes, Red Hot Chili Peppers

Reggae Nights

King Jammy, Buju Banton, Sizzla, Snow

California Love (Part 1)

Boo-Yaa T.R.I.B.E, Del Tha Funky Homesapien, Coolio and MC Eiht

The MAGIC of Fashion: Las Vegas Revisited

Marc Ecko, Russell Simmons, Karl Kani and Carl Jones

To receive your free copy of New York State of Mind (Part 1) visit

behindthemusictales.com

I am only looking for your first name and email. Once you are set up on the list you will receive periodic emails with a link to the next In Their Own Words: Behind the Music Tales of Truth, Fiction & Desire Sampler. You can opt out at any time.

WHO IS HARRIS ROSEN?

Father. Son. Brother.

HARRIS ROSEN was born and resides in Toronto, Canada. For twenty years he self-published the national lifestyle magazine Peace! in Canada. He has interviewed hundreds of composers, artists, actors and athletes, including the Notorious B.I.G., Dr. Dre, Daft Punk, Eminem, Derek Jeter, Georges St. Pierre, Nirvana, Metallica, Chris Rock, Buju Banton, Beastie Boys, Kiss, Destiny's Child and Aaliyah to list a select few.

He has traveled to six continents and was in the midst of a whirlwind of multiple musical cultural revolutions that occurred throughout the 90's and 2000's, while compiling a true and honest archive of audio, images and video.

Twitter: @MrHeller1
Facebook: https://www.facebook.com/NWAbook &
https://www.facebook.com/peacemagazine/
http://behindthemusictales.com/series-books/

N.W.A:
The Aftermath

EXCLUSIVE INTERVIEWS
WITH DR. DRE, ICE CUBE, JERRY HELLER, YELLA &
WESTSIDE CONNECTION

HARRIS ROSEN

ART BY BEN KINKEAD

IN THEIR OWN WORDS
BEHIND THE MUSIC TALES OF TRUTH, FICTION & DESIRE

Published by Peace! Carving

3rd edition

First published in July 2015

This edition first published in April 2016

ISBN: 978-0-9812587-0-6

Mr. Heller Press

Heller HQ

QB

Spadina-Fort York

Toronto, ON m5v 2b3

Canada

DEDICATION

This series is dedicated to my son Louis, late father, mother, sister, grandmother & the late Raymond Wallace.

Thank you for a lifetime of support and encouragement. I would not be here without you.

ACKNOWLEDGMENTS

I wish to personally thank the following people for their contributions to my inspiration and knowledge and other help in creating this book: Mark Reed, Rob Harris, Peter Cherniawski, Joey DAMMIT!, Ian Steaman, Eon Sinclair Jr., Sean Morgan, Todd DeKoker, Del Cowie, Martin Popoff, Sarah Stanners, Phil Demetro, James Watt, Chandler Bolt, John Tighe, Seven30 Bryce, William J. Genereux, Peter Lazanik, Rishi Persaud.

Contents

EAST COAST WEST COAST KILLAS

PREFACE

DR. DRE: *Tupac never knew me.*

ICE CUBE: *I just do shit for Ice Cube fans, not for Hip-Hop fans.*

YELLA: *Me and Dre produced all Eazy, N.W.A. All of that. Me and him did that together.*

JERRY HELLER: *There are people that think that I am the white Devil.*

N.W.A: The Aftermath is comprised of direct quotes from two exclusive Dr. Dre interviews, three exclusive Ice Cube interviews, one exclusive Yella interview, one exclusive Jerry Heller interview, one exclusive Westside Connection interview, and the press conference for Bow Down at Priority Records HQ.

They had all moved in different directions since N.W.A. Some were in different groups or running their own crew, while others had embarked on solo careers. Yet they were all still tied in some way to the West Coast Hip-Hop legacy of N.W.A. And that meant, they were inevitably still tied to controversy.

In a rare and vintage interview from 1996, Dr. Dre relayed deep unfiltered thoughts in the midst of his war with Death Row Records, shortly after the murder of Tupac Shakur. He spoke on his departure from N.W.A and Ruthless Records, Death Row Records, the beginning of Aftermath Entertainment, and laid out future plans. He went in on Snoop Doggy Dogg's Tha Doggfather, and responded to personal rumours.

In an exclusive 1999 interview prior to the release of Chronic 2001, a focused and balanced Dr. Dre marked his return to the top, while discussing his state of mind, karma, and spirituality, and explained why he said, "Fuck Rap".

In 2001, 2003, and 2006 exclusive interviews, and a 1996 press conference, Ice Cube spoke on hardcore Hip-Hop, New York City media, his battles with B-Real and Cypress Hill and Common, the explosive diss song "No Vaseline", both his film and music career while on the set of Friday After Next, and his passion for the Los Angeles Lakers and Oakland Raiders.

In a rare and vintage exclusive 1996 interview with Yella, the most misunderstood member of N.W.A, he spoke on the magic of the group and what led them to part ways. The mysterious death of his close friend Eazy-E, his relationships with Dr. Dre, Ice Cube and Ren, Ruthless Records, and the legacy of N.W.A.

In an exclusive 2006 interview inside his home, Jerry Heller, the most disrespected Manager in the history of the music business, responded to all questions and held nothing back. Putting his record up against anyone, he addressed his reputation as a crook, people who sent diss songs in his direction, and what happened when he came to face The Game. He spoke at length on what led him to meet up with Eazy-E, the rise and fall of Ruthless Records, and the final days of Eazy-E. And he named his selections to star in the film that has now become Straight Outta Compton.

Combined, the interviews provide a first-hand history of N.W.A with a view to the future and a key look into the state of mind of these legendary figures, who existed within the heart of arguably the most infamous and dark period in modern contemporary music history, in which lives were tragically lost.

Much of what you will read here has been sensationalized by others in a manner of journalistic psycho-speak. N.W.A: The Aftermath is as close to the truth as one can get. It delivers raw thoughts by real people and is manifested directly in the voice and words of the artists who made it happen.

Each chapter will unravel tall tales and give you new insight. Don't miss out on the opportunity to learn what really happened.

behindthemusictales.com

facebook.com/NWAbook

DISCLAIMER

Opinions expressed in the linked interviews are not necessarily those of the Author.

photo by Harris Rosen
Jerry Heller's home October 22, 2006 Calabasas, Ca

CHAPTER 1
IN THE BEGINNING

Jerry Heller released his tell all Ruthless: A Memoir in August 2006. A first-hand account of his life as a "super-agent" responsible for booking colossal tours for the likes of Elton John, Pink Floyd, Marvin Gaye, The Guess Who, Journey and many others. Then as the force behind Eric "Eazy-E" Wright, Ruthless Records, N.W.A and the West Coast Gangster Rap revolution.

A lot has been said and written about Jerry Heller since he first came to light as the man behind the grand vision of the late Eazy-E and the Ruthless Records empire. His name and character assailed more than any other single person or entity ever since he first parted ways with Ice Cube, then Dr. Dre, and eventually Eazy-E in the final days of his life. If you believe the infamous personal and spiritual diss songs and public comments directed his way, Jerry Heller is the biggest crook of all time. According to them, he and Eazy shaved points – and millions of dollars – off royalties they were owed from the multi-platinum sales of N.W.A.

Relaxing at his home on a sunny afternoon in Calabasas, California, where he lived at the time with his ex-wife and former Baywatch actress, Gayle Steiner, the then 66 year old veteran mogul of the American music industry said he couldn't care less. Maybe that's because he has thick skin, especially when it comes to the often cut-throat business of the music industry.

During the 1960's and 1970's, Heller was one of the top agents in the game. As well as being responsible for bringing Elton John and Pink Floyd to America, his roster of clients read like a who's who of the classic era. War, Average White Band, Marvin Gaye, Otis Redding, Journey, Styx, REO Speedwagon, Boz Scaggs, The Grass Roots, The Standells, The Guess Who, Joan Armatrading, Credence Clearwater Revival, Ike & Tina Turner, Van Morrison. Needless to say, he knows how to work records and the people who record them.

That track record led Eric Wright, aka Eazy-E, to meet with him one day in 1987. And the rest, as they say, is history: Ruthless Records was formed; N.W.A blew up Rap like never before; everybody became famous; some struck it rich; there were accusations of financial trickery; Cube left; Dr. Dre left, and the group split up; Cube and Dre recorded diss songs; Eazy-E died of AIDS related complications in 1995; and Heller went on to Hispanic Rap at Hit-a-Lick Records.

Or is it history? In *Ruthless: A Memoir*, the book written with Gil Reavill and published by Simon & Schuster, Jerry Heller finally decided to speak up and out about life and business among Eazy-E, Ice Cube, Dr. Dre and the rest of the Ruthless family in the late 1980's. Not one to put a mic in his hand, it served as his late-response record.

Jerry Heller: Let's go back to Sgt. Pepper and The Beatles. So, the album that I consider one of the two most important albums of the second half of the twentieth century; Sgt. Pepper and Straight Outta Compton. Sgt. Pepper set the bar so impossibly high for everybody else in the world that it because impossible to do an album that was competitive or that people thought was competitive, without spending so much money that people's jobs depended upon albums being successful. So it took the fact that people should be in the music business because they love music and what it put into it was an element of putting out records and promoting them just because they cost a lot of money rather than because you love music. So I just feel it's ironic that Sgt. Pepper, this great work of art was responsible for all that. So we now go through the new wave age of the 70s, the funk of the early 80s of which, of course, I was involved in.

The music business is the only win-win business that I have ever seen. It's the only business where... Normally in a business when you make more somebody else makes less. That's not true in the music business. In the music business, the more the artist makes, the more everybody makes. And that's a wonderful thing and I call that the economic integrity of the music business because everybody gets rich off an Alanis Morissette record, not just Alanis Morissette. Everybody does; the Publisher, the writers, the Producer, the record company. I mean, everybody's career was built on Jagged Little Pill and so obviously, that's a wonderful thing.

So when we did Straight Out Compton, well, first let me just set the stage here. I heard about a little scene that was happening at a pressing plant in Hollywood called Macola Records and it took me a couple of months to get over there. A friend of mine that I had done business with over the years, he had brought me Hugh Masekela and Miriam Makeba and Charlie Musselwhite. He's an old Blues guy and I trusted what he said. He said, "Look, there's a scene happening, I don't like it, I don't understand it." Not necessarily that he didn't like it, he didn't understand it, but maybe you'll like it. So I go over there and for a thousand dollars, you could press up 500 records and this guy would send it out to his friends and if by some freak of nature they played it on the one radio station in the world on this planet that played Rap music, which was a 5,000 watt station at the top of Alvarado Street called KDAY with Julio G and Tony G and Greg Mack; The Mix Masters, the record would start to sell.

So I went over there and at this little place were the L.A. Dream Team and J. J. Fad and Ice-T and MC Hammer and the World Class Wreckin' Cru and the Egyptian Lover and Rodney O & Joe Cooley and the Timex Social Club and Bobby Jimmy & the Critters, and they were all pressing at this little pressing plant. And if you sold 10,000 records, somebody went over to the back and cashed your cheque for 25,000 bucks and everybody split it up and I said, "This is what the music business... This is the basis of the music business. This movement is going to reestablish the economic integrity of the music business and this is what the music business is about."

Jerry Heller: So I signed a couple of the acts. The L.A. Dream Team and J.J. Fad, who recorded for Dream Team Records, and then I met Alonzo Williams and signed the World Class Wreckin' Cru and C.I.A., which was Sir Jinx and Cube, and Alonzo and I became good friends, and he kept telling me about this guy that wanted to meet me named Eric Wright. And at that time, even though I was very disenchanted with the music business, I certainly was a bigger name in the music business than anybody that recorded there.

Jerry Heller: It was a very bad time in my life personally, as well as a bad time in the music business. So Alonzo keeps telling me about this guy that wants to meet me, Eric Wright, and finally I agreed after a couple of months. I agreed to meet him because if I met everybody, every guy that wanted to be in business with me, that's all I would do is be in the business of meeting guys to be in business. So he gets out of the car; he drives up in a little Suzuki Samurai with MC Ren and he gets out of the car and he was an impressive little dude. He was very impressive, powerful and charismatic. He just had this thing. He was preternaturally clean and he just had an aura about him that got your attention. He was only 5" tall, 5"1, maybe 5"2. And I said to him "You've got anything that —". First of all, he reached in his sock and paid Alonzo $750 that he had paid him to meet. So I said, "You got anything to play?"

Now, I found certain things over my years in the music business. See, being around for a long time gives you an advantage, it's not a disadvantage because there are very few things that are new and if you've been there before and you have any brains at all, you know how to get there again. So when guys start telling you about what they've got "And I've got this guy, and I've got this chick, and this is my boy, and this is my group, and this is my girl and I've got this" and it's all bullshit. Let's just fucking talk. It's bullshit. In the agency business or in business as in general, when you say to a person, "Look, this is the cost of this," whether it's Marvin Gaye or whatever, and they say, "Money's no problem." Well, that's ridiculous. Money is always the problem, Normally, it's the only problem but it's always a problem and anyone that tells you that it isn't a problem is either the Sultan of Brunei's son or just full of shit; he has no money. I've had a million guys driving Mercedes 500 telling me that money is no problem and then asking me for two dollars to pay the valet to get his car when we go outside. So it's just like in Poker, they call it a tell, to me those are just tells. Anyone says that to you they're basically full of shit.

So I said, "You got anything to play to me?" and he just looked at me and he said, "Yeah." So right then and there, I knew that this was a no-bullshit, no-nonsense kind of guy willing to let the music do the talking, not telling what he'd done or who he has or how he was going to do it, you know. He just said, "Yeah." So we went inside and while we were in one room Ren was carving his initials into the guy; the owner of Macola's desk. He just thought he would do that because he was bored. But Eazy played me "Boyz-N-The-Hood" and I think the fact that I was 44 or 45 at the time, and had grown up knowing who Gil Scott-Heron was and The Last Poets and The Rolling Stones and especially The Black Panthers, that I said to myself, "Wow!" When someone can make me say wow, they've got something that's worth getting into. It's very hard to make me say wow! And the wow factor in music is an important factor and I think that anyone is successful is had to have said it. I'm sure that Irving (Azoff) said it when he heard The Eagles for the first time. I'm sure that Albert Grossman said it when he heard Janis Joplin and Bob Dylan for the first time. So I think it's an important thing, the wow factor. And this made me say wow because it was a combination of Gil Scott-Heron, The Rolling Stones, The Last Poets and The Black Panthers and I said to myself, "This is the first time that the voice of our inner cities is really gonna be heard".

Eazy-E - "Boyz-N-The-Hood" (https://youtu.be/RwPMKozHPCM)

So the focus of my job then switched from finding the music, which I knew there was no question in my mind that this was the most important music that I had heard since the beginning of Rock 'N Roll, to how to get it accepted by a white middle-class America. So that the whole focus of my focus then changed in my mind. Eazy and I made a deal. I called a meeting with of all my clients at this mob restaurant where Don Hunter and I used to get drunk all the time called Martoni's. I told them that I wasn't going to be... I couldn't represent them anymore unless they were gonna record for Ruthless and if they wanted to they could have a home in Ruthless, 'cause Eazy had already named the company, and otherwise I couldn't represent them. So I was willing to start all over at this point just because of this music that I had heard.

People from everywhere gather around
Checkin' out the sound that Eazy is throwin' down
With some help from Ren and Dre
Makin' a way with dope style
Yo Eazy, what ya gotta say

Eazy-E *"We Want Eazy"*

CHAPTER 2
THE RISE OF N.W.A & RUTHLESS RECORDS

Antoine "Yella" Carraby is the most misunderstood member of N.W.A. He came up with Dr. Dre as a local DJ and was enlisted alongside him by Alonzo Williams to become a member of electro sensations World Class Wreckin' Cru. Then Dre parted ways with Williams to start N.W.A. N.W.A released the "Panic Zone" single on August 13, 1987 and the N.W.A and the Posse compilation followed on November 6, 1987. By then, Dre had invited Yella into the group with the duo combining forces to co-produce Straight Outta Compton and Eazy-Duz-It in 1988, 100 Miles and Runnin' in 1990, and EFIL4ZAGGIN in 1991.

N.W.A - "Panic Zone"
(https://youtu.be/Xx_JQe6THkM)

During this period, Yella also contributed production and mixing work for Ruthless Records artists, J.J. Fad, Michel'le, The D.O.C. and others. Undeniably overshadowed by Dre, Yella's contributions were intrinsic to the success of N.W.A and all that followed in their wake, and his rise through the N.W.A arguably may even qualify as the X factor that quite possibly sparked their success.

On the heels of Dre's departure for Death Row Records, Yella remained Eazy's loyalist friend and solider and marked key contributions to Eazy's solo releases and Bone Thugs-N-Harmony. A soft-spoken man who preferred to let his music do the talking, he stayed neutral when his friends Andre "Dr. Dre" Young and Eric "Eazy-E" Wright took to disrespecting each other in public.

In the exclusive 1996 interview, Yella laid out what made N.W.A special, how he handled his business with Ruthless Records, and reaffirmed his contributions to the group.

Yella: I think it's because we came out so different in the beginning and so real. People appreciate stuff that's real. You know, like natural, nothing phony. We was doing music because we was doing music. Not for money. We was just doing it, and what we talked about was so real that they can relate to. I guess we came out so different that's the only reason I can see.

Jerry Heller: First of all, you don't build companies like Ruthless by accident. I mean, whatever part I played, it's like the Detroit Tigers. I don't know one guy in the Detroit Tigers team but they got a team and that team is successful and they beat some good ball clubs to get into the World Series and now they're playing St. Louis, so something works at that team. Things worked at Ruthless and part of those things were because of what he brought to the table, part of it were what I brought to the table and part of it was that we were fortunate enough to have the most talented guys in the history of Rap music. I mean, it's hard to miss when you've got Dr. Dre doing the beats for every song that ever came out on your label. Also, we implemented some things that people just don't do. We did one record at a time. Everybody worked on it. All the best people worked on the record, and then when we were done we turned it over to our distribution company and we started the next record. So there is some kind of genius behind where we were. We paid for everything ourselves. We didn't mortgage ourselves.

Yella: When Eric was around it was just me and him. He asked me, "What do you want?" And I said, "I don't know?" There wasn't any sort of contracts or nothing. That was just... To me that's real. If you can —

To me, it's still a business if you got to have contracts and stuff; somebody's going to be fucking each other. I mean, if you could negotiate all that before a contract, say, "All right, let's just have this just to have it." Then that's business. Nowadays it's woo... I don't know.

Jerry Heller: *It was just a really good situation with really talented people and that's why every record that we put out for a long time until Dr. Dre left; and even though we had some big records after Dre left, things changed because all you had to do to sign to Ruthless was tell Eazy that Dre wanted to sign you.*

Yella: *I always produced. Me and Dre produced all Eazy, N.W.A. All of that. Me and him did that together. You know that Dre just happened to rap and be seen a little more. Now that he blew up doing it on his own because I could have went with him but I didn't want to. I said, 'Nah, you do your own thing.' But you know, it wasn't, yeah...*

CHAPTER 3
NO VASELINE

N.W.A went on an unprecedented roll following the release of Straight Outta Compton in August 1988 all the way through to the summer of 2001 on the strength of their second album, EFIL4ZAGGIN, when it all fell apart. However, the chinks in the seemingly impenetrable armour began to be exposed for all to see in December 1989, when their top gun lyricist, Ice Cube, left over perceived royalty disputes.

Unable to work with his former partner, Dr. Dre, the bonafide top Producer on the west coast, Ice Cube set to work on his solo debut and headed back to Dre's cousin Sir Jinx, with whom he had previously shared a group called C.I.A. Then to the east coast where he enlisted the visionary Bomb Squad: Hank Shocklee, Keith Shocklee, Chuck D, Eric "Vietnam" Sadler, and Gary G-Wiz - who were responsible for crafting the hard innovative revolutionary sounds of Public Enemy. AmeriKKKa's Most Wanted dropped on May 16, 1990 and instantly marked Cube's dynamic entry as a solo artist capturing the hearts and minds of the nation and selling over 1 000 000 copies within two months.

Cube quickly sent another volley to his growing and hungry fan base with the release of the Kill at Will EP on July 1, 1990. N.W.A finally revolved from Straight Outta Compton and the departure of Ice Cube with the long-awaited 100 Miles and Runnin' EP on August 14, 1990 and lashed out at Ice Cube on the title track and "Real Niggaz", where they infamously branded him Benedict Arnold. When N.W.A returned with EFIL4ZAGGIN on May 28, 1991, selling 954 000 copies its first week and landing at number one on the Billboard Top 200 in week 2, it came stocked with the interlude "Message to B.A." directed at Ice Cube. He did not take it lightly.

Jerry Heller and The D.O.C. Dissing & Clowning Ice Cube (https://youtu.be/Iyun6fnPYls)

Ice Cube had something dark and deadly up his sleeve, and when he unleashed his sophomore solo album Death Certificate on October 29, 1991 shit hit the fan. Its knee-jerk racial and class prejudices captured the rage and frustration of a nation of millions who were fed up with the state of America in the months leading up to the 1992 Los Angeles riots. The directive no holds barred iterations on anyone and everyone who stood in his way or that of his beloved core of Black listeners. The alleged bigotry of Korean merchants, who operated stores within Black districts of Los Angeles on "Black Korea"; homosexuals, pop rappers, the Chief of the L.A.P.D., Black people in interracial relationships; and inevitably his personal response to the harsh words his former N.W.A compatriots sent his way, which he addressed on the explosive diss song reply, "No Vaseline."

"No Vaseline" was instantaneously labelled anti-Semitic for its antagonistic attack on Jerry Heller. It marked the first time revered music industry trade publication Billboard condemned an artist in its editorial, stating Death Certificate represented "the rankest sort of racism and hate mongering." Jewish human rights group, the Simon Wiesenthal Centre, called for its removal from four music retail chains, and the UK stripped both "Black Korea" and "No Vaseline" from its version of the release.

In the exclusive 2006 interview with Jerry Heller, he expressed his feelings on the song, its impact on him, and what ensued following its release. During the 1996 Westside Connection press conference, Ice Cube was asked to comment on the song too.

Ice Cube - "Black Korea"
(https://youtu.be/iFwA0UwnuS8)

Ice Cube - "No Vaseline"
(https://youtu.be/bvRc7pwnt0U)

Jerry Heller: I think that it probably hurt me and affected me more than anything that's ever been said or done to me. I mean, I grew up in an era of anti-Semitism, you know. I grew up in the Mid-West, went to school in the Mid-West and then came out to USC where there was also rampant anti-Semitism. But I thought it was a terrible, terrible song. I think that it's the most anti-Semitic song that I have ever heard. I think that he's not anti-Semitic. I think that he did it just because he thought it will sell records, just like he did "Black Korea". I don't think that he has that kind of intestinal fortitude within him to be; I think he's, rather than being anti-Semitic, I just think he's just pro-Ice Cube, he'll do whatever it takes to put Ice Cube, to get him ahead. So it sort of put it in a different perspective for me but I just think it's a terrible song. Rabbi Cooper and Rabbi Hier from the Wiesenthal Centre came out and declared it anti-Semitic and said that Ice Cube was an anti-Semite and I sort of felt good that without; I didn't know them and they just came out and said it. It sort of vindicated how I felt a little. But Ice Cube, to me, is, that's just the way he is. I think that everything he says has a purpose. He's very bright, comes from a very bright family, he is well educated. And I think that everything he says has a purpose and that purpose is to move him ahead in the world, so you have to take it for what it is.

Ice Cube: It was from the heart, you know. That was from the heart. I mean like, truly like pissed off, like right and mad from the heart. And I wrote that record right after I heard the diss — that they dissed me. Same with Cypress Hill, same with Common Sense. It's like soon as I hear it I got to write.

photo by Harris Rosen
Post 2nd annual BET Awards June 24, 2002 Kodak Theatre, Los Angeles, Ca

CHAPTER 4
THE END OF N.W.A

Marion Hugh Knight Jr., aka Suge Knight, earned his reputation as a fierce Football player and track star. In 1987 he played two games for the Los Angeles Rams during the player's strike before working as a concert promoter and bodyguard for the likes of Bobby Brown. Unfortunately, his life began to unravel in October 1987 when he went off and was charged with domestic violence for cutting his girlfriend's ponytail in the street, and for auto theft, carrying a concealed weapon, and attempted murder on Hallow's Eve in Las Vegas. In late 1988 and early 1989 Knight served as a $70 a day bodyguard for Ruthless Records. He formed his own publishing company in 1989 and went to the wall for clients, infamously hanging Vanilla Ice out of a hotel room balcony by his ankles in order to coerce the rapper to sign over royalties to mega-hit "Ice Ice Baby" for its usage of his client Mario Johnson, aka Chocolate, material.

In the fall of 1990, Suge Knight started a management company and signed DJ Quik and The D.O.C. Upon reviewing D.O.C.'s contract, Knight singled out Jerry Heller for financial impropriety, cajoled The D.O.C. to address it with his friend Dr. Dre. In his book Ruthless: A Memoir, Jerry Heller states that Knight showed up at the office of Ruthless lawyer Ira Selsky and demanded Dr. Dre's employment contract and those of The D.O.C. and Michel'le. Shortly thereafter, Suge and three of his goons made an impromptu menacing appearance inside Heller's office. Heller responded by retaining the service of ex-Mossad agent Mike Klein, who Eazy-E later made Director of Business Affairs. Knight's strategy then switched to heavy breathing late night death threat calls to Heller and occasionally tailing Eazy-E through South Central.

On March 18, 1991, Eazy-E and Jerry Heller infamously attended Republican President George H.W. Bush's Inner Circle luncheon at the White House. On April 23, 1991 Eazy-E showed up at Galaxy Studio on the invitation of Dr. Dre to settle their differences but was infamously met by Suge Knight and his goons and forced at gunpoint to sign release papers for Dr. Dre, The D.O.C. and Michel'le, however he signed a fake signature. By then Heller had relocated to a gated community in Calabasas Valley but it was not protected from Suge Knight. On July 4, 1991 he arrived home to find his $150 000 Corvette missing and his home burgled with the message "Payback's a motherfucker, Jerry." scrawled on his bathroom mirror. Heller and his wife immediately relocated to the Four Seasons as a $75 000 security system was installed in their home.

***The Beef they didn't show in the Straight Outta Compton Movie Part 1
(https://youtu.be/RbgTlcZSO5U)***

***The Beef they didn't show in the Straight Outta Compton Movie Part 2
(https://youtu.be/eFxschmZIHQ)***

***The Beef they didn't show in the Straight Outta Compton Movie part 3
(https://youtu.be/mUerMeqY3Fk)***

In November 1991, Dr. Dre came to Eazy-E "crying" for Christmas money and promptly met with Eazy's rebuke. Jerry Heller responded by cutting Dre a $40 000 cheque only to be called a "damn sucker" by Eazy. Heller then jumped into action to save the day and working relationship with Ruthless's workhorse producer, Dr. Dre. In Ruthless: A Memoir, Heller claims to have brokered a $20 000 000 deal with Irving Azoff and Warner Bros, with an immediate $2 000 000 payment to Dr. Dre. However, due to the controversial message of N.W.A and Ice-T's "Cop Killer" song, the deal was vetoed by Warner Bros. Records President Mo Ostin. A sit down at a law office ensued, during which Eazy stared into the eyes of Dre who wore sunglasses, but nothing was resolved and Dr. Dre was free to co-found Death Row Records with The D.O.C. and Suge Knight.

Eazy-E, Jerry Heller and in turn the entire Ruthless Records roster was then under siege by both Ice Cube and Dr. Dre. In April 1992, Dr. Dre and Snoop Doggy Dogg released the title track for the undercover cop saga, Deep Cover soundtrack, starring Laurence Fishburne and Jeff Goldblum. It blew up instantly and overnight Snoop Doggy Dogg was proclaimed a star. By the time Dr. Dre released his essential classic The Chronic on December 15, 1992, distributed by Priority Records, Ruthless Records and Death Row Records were at war with multiple diss songs coming fast and furious most notably directed at both Eazy-E and Jerry Heller on "Fuck wit Dre Day."

Dr. Dre and Snoop Doggy Dogg - Fuck with Dre Day (And Everybody's Celebratin') (https://youtu.be/YyMeweFrT_s)

Ironically, when Death Row Records was being courted by Jimmy Iovine's Interscope Records, a behind the scenes agreement was hammered out with Jerry Heller, in order to avoid a lawsuit, that paid Ruthless Records 10% of all Dre's production monies, 15% of his album sales and a "huge" advance. Eazy and Jerry then upped the ante by retaining the services of notorious gang members and rappers, B.G. Knocc Out and Gangsta Dresta. Ruthless Records then inked a new distribution agreement with Relativity Records, wherein they maintained ownership of master recordings, and Eazy went in super hard on Dre with It's On (Dr. Dre) 187um Killa on October 19, 1993 touching him on every track, notably "Real Muthaphuckkin G's."

B.G. Knocc Out - Dr. Dre Set Up Eazy-E In Suge Knight Altercation (https://youtu.be/uu-62LPWU4w)

EAZY-E - "Real Muthaphuckkin G's" - HD DIRECTOR'S CUT - Explicit (https://youtu.be/car_j3HFELE)

It was a messy affair that captured the attention of the entire music community at large. Yella and Jerry Heller discussed what led to the end of N.W.A in their exclusive 1996 and 2006 interviews with a special appearance from the exclusive 1996 Dr. Dre interview.

Yella: *Hmmm, I think the reason why it broke up really was there was about to be too much money. To me, that's what I think the real reason was. Too much money. Not enough but too much. And when you start making too much money outside people always start interfering with the inside. Outside people telling people this, and that's how you get a breakup 'cause was nobody being cheated or nothing like that. It was all coming from outside people.*

Dr. Dre: *Actually, at the beginning I wasn't running my business. I'm a young kid out of Compton. The only thing I was interested in is making Hip-Hop music. That's all. I had some people doing my business which is a very big mistake, which was a very big mistake, and I got jerked, straight up. To be perfectly honest, I was getting two points for my production and a motherfucker could come off the street and get four. This is after I had made a couple of platinum records and I went to Eazy with an ultimatum. 'Get rid of the fucking Manager, Jerry Heller, or I'm leaving. Take a pick.' He chose to stay with Jerry Heller and I bounced and went to Death Row.*

Yella: *Nah, it's just people on the outside that had nothing to do with the group. Always. But if somebody in your ear, "You know, you should get this", or "You should be better", something like that, you start listening to them. So that drives people away. All the time. And then most groups break up because of money. But most of the time its because of somebody cheating. In this situation it was just starting to be too much money.*

Jerry Heller: It changed the dynamics of everything. But I gotta tell you, I think Dre is the single most talented person of the last 20 years. This guy is at the very top of his game. He was making hits for the Wreckin' Cru in 1986 and he's making the biggest records in the world today and he gets my vote, man. This guy is the most talented person of the Rap era. And I feel a kind of pride in that.

Yella: I don't like stuff that's going on between Dre and Eric. I tell Eric, I used to tell him all the time, I don't want to do none of the dissing because I have nothing against him. I just stay more neutral then anything and people can appreciate being neutral. Not "Oh, you was on his side or this side", even though I was still with Eazy, but I just kept my mouth quiet. It was none of my business.

I just happened to stick with him because Eric did nothing bad to me, so I stayed true. You know, so Eric appreciated it all the way up to his grave. I stood there, never turned my back, nothing. Even when he was going through all the bad times. All of the hanging out with... you know. Never turned my back. Always there.

Jerry Heller: There are people that think that I am the white Devil, which is so ironic because when Eazy and I started the company on March 3rd of 1987, you know, I said, "Well, we're gonna make sure that the traditional roles of people in the music business aren't the same. We're gonna make sure that nobody ever talks about Ruthless the same way they talked about Morris Levy and Jackie Wilson and Nat Tarnopal and Bo Diddley and Little Richard, you know. They are gonna talk about you the way they talk about Berry Gordy. You are going to be the great savior of the music business".

And when it all comes down to it I'll put my record up against anybody's in the history of this business. I founded the biggest acts in the world, not only that, every act that I've been involved with is as big today as they were when I discovered them. And if Eazy was alive today and N.W.A were here, they'd be selling out stadiums the same as the Rolling Stones do. Basically, when it's all said and done that's how we're judged. I don't play any instrument, so I can only be judged by the people I've represented.

Like I told Elton John at Santa Monica Civic one night, which was his first date outside of the Club Troubadour, a club-like environment. We were standing out in the audience watching the opening act and I said, "I can put you in the right place at the right time, in front with the right audience. Once the house lights goes down, I'm the same as everybody else that paid $12.50 to see you, it's you and them." So that about sums it up.

I write this book and a friend of mine, Reggie Turner, who is in prison right now, said to me, "In my world, if you don't deny something, people thinks it's true." I said, "That's the most ridiculous thing I have ever heard." He said, "For you to say that is naïve and arrogant because what I'm telling you is the truth of the streets and you don't know what the fuck you're talking about." So I thought about that for a while and it turned out that he was absolutely right and I was absolutely wrong.

I thought to myself, okay now, Ice Cube leaves N.W.A. Now let's just think about this logically. Eazy had the key to this house, he lived two house down and he used to come over at 3:30 or 4:00 in the morning on his way home and I would get up at 4:00 to go to the office at 5:00 because that's when I can get the most work done before people came in with cocktail napkins and stuff saying that Eazy said that they could have $15 000 or $20 000 or whatever. I would hear him rambling around up there. (Heller pointed to the second floor of his home overlooking the living room) He would sit up there and I would have all of the day's correspondence, whatever it might be. I'd have cheques for him to sign. But I thought to myself, now, do these people think that Eazy and I used to sit up there and say "Let's see now, let's do the royalty statements now and fuck Ice Cube." Or, "Let's do these royalty statements and fuck N.W.A!"

I mean, do people really think that I would know how to do a royalty statement? I mean, it's ridiculous. Nobody could possibly believe that. But they did believe it and they do believe it. But, we had a business manager named Lester Knispel, K-N-I-S-P-E-L. He's the business manager for Barbra Streisand, Shaquille O'Neal, The Eagles, Irving Azoff, Phil Mickelson, almost every professional Golfer in the world, almost every professional Basketball player in the world, Paula Abdul, Rod Stewart for thirty years. We just tell Lester to fuck these guys, to cook the books and he would just do it? And then when the royalty statements came out and were checked by Bob Dudnick, who was the Senior Litigator at Paul Hastings Janofsky & Walker and Ira Selsky, our in-house guy that became a partner at Allen Grubman's, and then were sent to us to draw cheques and sign them and pay people. This is like, what, a Jewish conspiracy? To fuck the African-American musician? I mean, I say that's so ridiculous. And then when they get their cheques, Ice Cube had a lawyer named Lee Young, who was at one time the head of business affairs at Motown for Berry Gordy for many years, his father was before him. He represents Ice Cube to this days. Ice Cube's business manager was a guy named, I think, Fred Moultrie, who represented The Jackson 5. You think that these guys don't know how to read a royalty statement? That they just got these royalty statements and said, "Oh, Jerry and Eazy just sent these over so they have to be right."

We're talking about a 10 million dollar a month company and the most sophisticated people in the history of the music business and we screw these guys? Give me a fucking break. You wanna believe that I've got a bridge that I wanna sell you that connects Brooklyn with Manhattan. So, I never thought that that could happen. Also, I think it's quite unusual that for guys that got fucked so often that none of them every sued Ruthless, or Jerry Heller or Eric Wright, and that's a matter of public record. And if you care to do your homework you'll see that none of us, none of those entities were ever sued by anybody that said we stole money from them. That seems unusual to me for people that say they got screwed out of millions of dollars.

I think Ice Cube took this position 'cause it's a traditional position in the music business, the white man stole from him and especially the white Jew stole from him, and I think that he stuck with that position so long there's no chance that he believes it. He just, that's his position, so to this day I say to him, "Get a fucking life!" Guy's worth probably 150 or 200 million dollars; he is the single, most successful Black movie entrepreneur since Spike Lee, not as an Actor. I'm talking about as a Producer and creator of films because in the movie business, you have very few Spielberg' and very few George Lucas' where people have a continuing relationship with them. Usually it's one movie with an actor who is playing the part one time, basically, and it's not like the music business where you have Joni Mitchell on her 13th album or Billy Joel on his 27th album or whatever it is. You basically don't have those kinds of relationships. And Ice Cube, his movies come in for low budgets and under budgets and they do big numbers and he's an important, important guy in the film business. I don't think he sold a record probably in the last three albums.

CHAPTER 5
THE END OF THE LINE FOR JERRY HELLER

Jerry Heller sat in the Ruthless Records hot seat from the time of Ice Cube's departure until he was eventually sent legal notice that his services were no longer required in February 1995. He had withstood countless personal and alleged physical attacks; however, the undying desire of Eazy-E to reform N.W.A trumped all. And the involvement of Jerry Heller in any way, shape, manner or form stopped any and all talks immediately.

There is definitely a lot of grey area surrounding this time. Ruthless Records had turned the corner, following the departure of Dr. Dre, selling millions of Eazy-E solo releases, and their new crop of artists led by the success of Bone Thugs-N-Harmony appeared promising. Their EP Creepin On Ah Come Up, released on June 21, 1994, had sold over two million copies, and they were putting in work on what became E. 1999 Eternal, which went on to sell over five million copies, hitting number one on the Billboard Top 200 chart and earning the group a 1996 Grammy Award for Best Rap Recording nomination.

Behind the scenes, Eazy-E was spending more time with Tomica Woods, who he begun dating in 1991 and shared a son, Dominick. Woods had a background in the music business as secretary to Tabu

Records founder, Clarence Avant, and joined Avant when he was named Chairman of Motown Records in 1993. Avant is portrayed as the bad guy in the acclaimed Searching for Sugar Man documentary on Sixto Rodriguez. He is known as the Godfather of Black Music, who managed Sarah Vaughan, Jimmy Smith, and Lalo Schifrin; presided over Venture Records, Sussex Records, and Tabu Records, signing the likes of Bill Withers, Kool & The Gang, SOS Band, and Jimmy Jam & Terry Lewis; and several entrepreneurial projects.

Eazy-E was checked into Cedars-Sinai Medical Centre on February 24, 1995, diagnosed with AIDS shortly thereafter, and remained in the hospital until his death on March 26, 1995. Woods, who was three months pregnant at the time (with his daughter Daijah), wed Eric "Eazy-E" Wright twelve days prior to his death in a beside ceremony. She then became known as Tomica Woods-Wright and inherited Ruthless Records and its value reputed to be $15 million.

Jerry Heller spoke on his final days with Eazy-E during the exclusive 2006 interview.

Jerry Heller: *Now as far as Eazy and I, Eazy and I didn't have a falling out, okay. It wasn't the first time in our relationship that we didn't talk to each other for a period of time. He did what he did, I did what I did and if he was doing something that I didn't like, he wouldn't come around. It started in November right before Thanksgiving of 1994 and there were a lot of people around him as happens when a company is enormously successful, just like it happened around The Jackson 5; pretty soon everybody had their own lawyer and everybody had their own agent, and everybody had their own publicist, that's what happens. And Eazy had stood up for me against Cube and Dre, Don King, Jesse Jackson, Clarence Avant and Minister Farrakhan. I mean, lots of people tried to take shots at Jerry Heller once they saw that Rap music was going to be what it became. I think that toward the end of 1994 a lot of people were in his ear. "Jerry's doing this" and "Jerry's doing that". "He's charging you too much and he's making more than you are" and whatever.*

Whatever they were telling him, I think that he was at the final stages of a terrible, terrible, debilitating, horrible death disease and he just didn't have the strength to just do it anymore. I think that whatever he thought to himself, it was; I think that he was thinking that it would be hard to have an N.W.A reunion with me around, so he would have to deal with that somehow because there is nothing that he wanted more in his life, nothing more than an N.W.A reunion. That was his all-consuming desire and I certainly would have moved to the background to facilitate something like that. I mean nothing would have made me happier than an N.W.A reunion.

I think that this disease had just devastated him to the point where it had affected his relationships and he went in to the hospital, I think, in January of '95. We finished the Bone album in August of '94. January of '95; went in the hospital. About that time I stopped coming to the office. In February of '95 I got a letter from him, supposedly from him, but people around him told me that he was in the hospital signing all kinds of blank documents and people filled in whatever they wanted to. I think on February 16th or 17th, that was the end of my relationship with Ruthless.

Photo by Harris Rosen
Post 2nd annual BET Awards June 24, 2002 Kodak Theatre,
Los Angeles, CA

CHAPTER 6
THE MYSTERIOUS DEATH OF EAZY-E

The death of Eric "Eazy-E" Wright took the world by storm. One moment he was actively involved in a war with Dr. Dre and Death Row Records and the next he was dead. Eazy-E was admitted to the hospital on February 24, 1995 and shortly thereafter diagnosed with AIDS. A public statement announcing his illness was released on March 16, 1995; a suspect final message to his fans followed a few days later; he succumbed to the disease on March 26, 1995 at the age of 31.

The rapid spread of the disease in his body has led many people to believe to this day that his death was the result of foul play. Eazy-E was known for enjoying multiple sex partners; however, none of them or any of his children tested positive for the HIV virus, most notably his daughter Daijah with Tomica Woods-Wright, who was born six months after his death. Many people are on record stating Eazy-E was injected with the virus during an acupuncture session.

Bone Thugs-N-Harmony have point blank named Jerry Heller as the culprit in multiple interviews, stating Eazy-E had a cough in December 1994 and January 1995 that quickly developed into pneumonia, to a HIV positive diagnosis in February, and then full blown AIDS and death in March. Going on to claim that Eazy-E had fired Jerry Heller post a meeting with Ice Cube, denoting that Cube broke down his understanding of Ruthless Records financials and detailed how Eazy could function on his own. Stating that Heller remained in the office post his firing, and that Eazy had a soft spot for him and declined to ask him to vacate. Layzie Bone tied it all together by suggesting it was Heller's Doctors Eazy visited. "I was kinda thinking like, who the fuck Doctors did he go to? I think it was Jerry Heller's Doctors that he went to and he had just got fired, so I'm like I don't know." Bold claims indeed, however holes in the theory appear when Bone tied the decline of Eazy to his 1991 appearance at the Republican White House luncheon with President George H.W. Bush, and suggested it was Jerry Heller who pushed for the deathbed marriage to Tomica Woods.

Bone Thugs-N-Harmony - The conspiracy behind the death of Eazy-E
(https://youtu.be/qtVLxraMtgk)

Kid Frost stated Eazy hurt himself in the Valley riding a Quad runner and it was a "person in rap", who was referred to as the Devil that referred him to an acupuncturist.

Kid Frost - Frost Says He Knows How Eazy-E Got HIV
(https://youtu.be/wnuhHzMmk4s)

The most popular tale is that Suge Knight orchestrated it behind the scenes. In a 2003 interview with Jimmy Kimmel, Knight casually mentioned Eazy-E and then chuckled: "They get blood from somebody with AIDS and they shoot you with it. So that's a slow death, an Eazy-E thing, you know what I mean?"

Suge Knight Talked About KILLING EAZY-E on Jimmy Kimmel
(https://youtu.be/31w2reSfxnY)

Yella and Jerry Heller spoke on the mystery behind the tragic loss. During the exclusive 1996 interview, Yella relayed his thought and feelings in regards to the untimely passing on his close friend. Jerry

Heller spoke on the loss of his dear friend and former business partner in his exclusive 2006 interview.

Yella: I knew the night before, that's when I found out. The night before the press conference. I knew it then, but he actually didn't write that last letter. He was already on the machine when I found out. So, I didn't get to even ask him — I didn't get to talk nothing about it. He only knew a few weeks before that. So it was like all a surprise.

Jerry Heller: There were people, lots of people that were around him then that said that he was signing lots of blank sheets of paper and things were being filled in afterwards. Just like I know that he didn't write that speech that his... they say long time lawyer who had been his lawyer for all of six weeks or something; Ron Sweeney read over the air that day on the radio. Eric would have never written something like that, it was just so out of character for him because he always said, "I'm not a fucking role model." So for him to write this kind of letter and then mistake the number of children he had and the number women that were their mothers. It just was bullshit. So I didn't take that seriously at all. That wasn't him.

Yella: Usually people die from that be sick looking... you know? He was nothing like that. I mean, it was like it just happened overnight and the funny thing about that — a couple of girls I knew he was with, none of them has the symptoms. Nothing, nobody has AIDS. So, you know... It's just some funny stuff. I don't know what, but it's something.

Jerry Heller: He died on March the 26th of '95 and I got nothing but ...

Yella: It could be different things, or the most unique AIDS that ever happened because I knew somebody that used to live on my street a long time ago had AIDS. It took them nine months to a year to die. They were skinny, you know, just sick and this was... woo! This is some very unique stuff. Like somebody put something in a vein or something. I really don't --- And an autopsy was never taken but you never know what can happen. If money is involved, anything can happen. Definitely anything can happen.

Jerry Heller: *Not a day goes by that I don't think about him and miss him. He was like my son and I do have a relationship with his daughter, Erin, EB, and her mother, Tracy. They were at our anniversary party the other night and Eazy was a special guy and certainly changed my life.*

Yella: *Every day above ground is a good day. People think, "Oh, I can't pay my bills, I can't pay this..." That is nothing. That is not that bad. Once you get under the ground, there's no more of that, you know? You got to enjoy life while you can. I think Eazy's death opened up the eyes — opened up the world's eyes. Let 'em know that AIDS, hey, that's real stuff, you know.*

There's a threat in the world today
A threat to our way of living, a threat to our
society
And maybe even a threat to our very existence
And what is this threat? The WESTSIDE
CONNECTION
An organization made up of highly motivated
Extremely aggressive gangstas turned businessmen
with one single objective
World domination, or in their words "Creating a
world wide Westside"
Vowing to make every man woman and child bow
down
To the "W", a hand sign used by their members to
show affiliation
We have confirmed reports that "W"'s have been
appearing on the various
Monuments and historical landmarks throughout
the world. There are also talks
Of Mount Rushmore being renamed Mount
Westmore, with America's forefathers
Being replaced by the WESTSIDE CONNECTION
forefathers, Ice Cube, WC, and Mack 10
A.k.a. The Gangsta, The Killa, and The Dope
Dealer
When confronted with these allegations they
released a statement saying...
Quote... "Bitch, you know the side, world
motherfucking wide."....... unquote

**Westside Connection –
"World Domination (Intro)"**

Issue #28 Fall 1996

CHAPTER 7
WESTSIDE CONNECTION BOW DOWN

n the thick of the east coast vs west-coast war, Ice Cube, never one to leave an opportunity to shine and earn dollars behind, banded together his friend and traveling hype man, W.C. and upcoming Inglewood artist, Mack 10 to record "Westside Slaughterhouse" for Mack 10's self-titled debut in June 1995. A response to the Common song "I Used to Love H.E.R.", where the rapper metaphorically connected the fall of conscious rap with the rise of gangster rap. The video featured Ice Cube, W.C. and Mack 10 roaming an abattoir covered in blood while dropping lyrical bombs and hovering over a tied up prisoner whom they appear to be served on a plate following his violent demise at its end.

Common Sense -"I Used To Love H.E.R."
(https://youtu.be/J1Dk-obLsiQ)

Mack 10, Ice Cube and W.C. - "Westside Salughterhouse"
(https://youtu.be/l8Y3LU2J3n0)

The crew revisited the concept a few months later for W.C.'s "West Up!" that was released as a single in August 1995 and included on his Curb Servin' album. The chemistry was tight, the demand was there, and so they proceeded to record a full-fledged album. The classic Westside Connection album Bow Down arrived on Priority Records on October 22, 1996. Dedicated to the health and welfare of a Hip-Hop nation hit hard by tax cuts, Westside Connection took no shorts in their quest to create a worldwide California love and, in turn, one Hip-Hop nation under a groove. Bow Down serving as a full frontal attack by the trio on anyone who stepped in their way or offended west coast Hip-Hop.

W.C. and the Maad Circle featuring Mack 10 and Ice Cube - "West Up!" (https://youtu.be/6B3lAj2S80o)

Prior to the release of the album, Westside Connection met with invited media inside Priority Records HQ for a press conference and select follow up interviews.

Ice Cube: We doing the record really to celebrate West Coast Hip-Hop and to; it's really dedicated to what we've done for Hip-Hop and what we doing out here in the west and to be recognized as a powerhouse in Hip-Hop and for it to be really, really one Hip-Hop nation under a groove. We thought it was definitely needed, that this Westside Connection album be put together by us and put out.

Malik Singleton: L.A. Weekly

In Source Magazine or in one single attraction it said Hip-Hop started in the west, you know? An infamous statement that got everybody off and one interesting thing we were discussing is how in a sense, just like as far as West Coast Hip-Hop goes, a lot of the influences that you see in a lot of West Coast Hip-Hop are from things that were not really started in the east. Things like; we all remember things like old Toddy Tee that we used to hear coming up and a lot of the music behind it goes back to like old '70s funk. So in a sense, I guess it's almost like that statement has validity that not everybody should top off about. Is that part of the message that you're trying to get through for Westside Connection.

Ice Cube: Well, in a sense, for us, when Hip-Hop started out here, it did start in the west for us because it was a new start. It was something *different for us. I think we truly made Hip-Hop real and we really want to talk about what's really going on and the pain that people are suffering everywhere, you know what I'm saying? Hip-Hop was the first one to say — I mean, west coast was the first one to say, "Fuck the Flash. Boom-boom, this that and the other." It's just all about here's how I'm livin', you know? And it became a style in Hip-Hop just like the Native Tongue or whatever. It became a style, so Hip-Hop did start in the west, you know what I'm saying? I'm just saying it 'cause it wasn't truly real until we started doing it... to us. We don't know about skyscrapers, we don't know about none of that stuff, you know? So it's only true when we start talking about our neighbourhoods, so that's what that statement really, truly means.*

I'd like to know what type of response you think this album is going to get from music audiences in general and the east coast.

Ice Cube: Well, we really — we didn't really make the record like thinking on people's response. We just kind of did something from the gut, that we love, that we want to hear. You know, I think Hip-Hop — if we talking about hardcore music, Hip-Hop needs a hardcore album that's just truly just rough, you know. I mean, you have some groups that's doing it, like Heltah Skeltah, you know what I'm saying? They have this truly rough record and I think Hip-Hop need that and I think Westside Connection is going to bring that to it. That's why we did the record. So I don't know what people want — how people gonna react. I just want people to understand why we did the record and why we put it out. And the true people who really, truly, truly looking for the righteous of answering this thing would know why we put the record out: because it was needed.

I'd like to hear from each one of you guys just about working together on this project, coming together for one single effort and just tell me a little bit maybe either something that happened in the studio or something about bonding together. You guys together — like you had said earlier in a previous interview that this is really something that you wanted to do and so now you guys are working together for this project, so tell me a little bit about that.

W.C.: *Well for me, W.C., I was called down to come to the studio to get down with my homeboy's song, Mack 10, "Slaughterhouse", and the chemistry was so good there that we decided to move on to my album and do "West Up!". And we was getting a lot of responses and stuff from something that we was truly feeling from the heart. A lot of people was finding it hard to swallow and we felt like if we were just putting it down on one or two songs like this, what could happen if we come out with a whole album? And the chemistry was so tight to where we said, "You know, let's start messing around and see what we come up with."*

I mean, we started going inside the studio putting it down and the chemistry started getting better and better and better and everybody was just feeling real comfortable to the point to where we just said, "Let's just go full-fledged with the album." I mean, originally it was Cube idea, whether if we could all get together and do this right here. We was already homeboys saying let's get on each other record, but as far as us just getting together and doing the whole project there was no problem. I mean, because we all cool with each other and everything and we all share the same views on a lot of different issues dealing with this Hip-Hop nation over here on the west coast. So that was no problem right there.

Mack 10: *It was the same way with me as like with Dub. The other songs turning out so good, so Cube was like, "What would happen if we did a whole album, you know what I'm saying?" But really, another thing, it was like a workout for us, you know what I'm saying? Because it was like a lot of friendly competition. You do a record by yourself, you ain't got nothing to test yourself against, you know what I'm saying? Second verse might not be hard as the first verse, but on this if you slack you was going to get ripped, you know what I'm saying? So it was like a workout for everybody to me. It was just all in fun to me, so that's that.*

Billy Johnson: Rap Sheet

My question is: to what extent do you guys feel you helped unify the west coast. I know that now everyone's throwing up the W's, so how do you guys feel about that?

Ice Cube: I think it was definitely needed. People got to understand something about the west coast. We love Rap, you know what I'm saying? But we also love money too even though we gonna try and get it both, so it was a lot of competition on the west coast. You had a lot of different cliques out here selling a lot of records. Sometimes — it was friendly competition. It was never anything bad about it like this clique and that clique making money but definitely we wanted people to buy our record before they bought anybody else's. That's just life, that's just how it be, but you got everybody throwing up the "dub" now which is good because we need to be unified and we need for everybody on the west coast to appreciate what we've contributed to the Hip-Hop nation and just love it and love what we doing, and not feel ashamed that we do Gangster Rap or, this record do this and y'all should stop and C. Dolores Tucker and all that shit that don't really mean nothing to the real world or mean nothing to us. You know, we stopped really caring about that and just started doing the records how we know is true.

Mack 10: But that W is our sign the whole way, you know what I'm saying? That's our hood. Westside Connection, that's how we affiliated ourselves. That's our hood, that's our sign. I don't know why everybody else is doing it. It's cool though because you can't get mad at nobody for liking what you doing and wanting to be a part of, but for us, that's our hood. Westside Connect or nothing, you know what I'm saying?

What part did Mack 10, Ice Cube, and Dub C play as far as making the album, Westside Connection?

Ice Cube: Well, I kind of just took the lead, really, on the record. We would all just bounce ideas. We decided to definitely get tracks from outside producers, so we didn't really have to concentrate on tracks, you know? We got QDIII, who's always helped me out in the past. We got this new kid named Budda, who's Sam Sneed's cousin and we got Binky, which is a guy from one of his groups called AllFrumTha I. So, we just concentrated really on making good material and making each record stand on its own, and not just have records that were thrown together. This project — when we started? Last year? End of last year, just putting it together and we got 10 songs that was tight. So that was kind of my role. I say I was like the glue and everybody else had different roles. I *think Dub made sure everything stayed as rough as possible with his contribution. So that was going to be his glitch, to make sure everything was rough as possible. Mack is just Superman, so, you know [Laughing]. Yeah, yeah, definitely. We all put in what we had to offer.*

Dub C, W.C. and tha Maad Circle coming from off the first album with Coolio, and then you came back with the second album. What did you think you had to put into this Westside Connection so you would really compare it like you're supposed to compare it?

W.C.: *Basically just rep and be myself. Come in and just — I mean, with this Westside Connection album I got a chance to show a side of me that wasn't showing — that really wasn't fully exposed on either one of my albums. I got a chance just to open up and to speak on different issues and stuff that wasn't spoke on in my albums which was cool because — I mean, when you doing an album, sometimes you got to stay within a realm to make sure that album is not going everywhere, and this album right here, we would send in different topics and stuff and I was able to say, "Damn, I wanted to get down on this topic right here on my last album but on this one right here I can just open up and do it." So I mean, all was me coming off my last two albums but on this one right here I can open up and do it — I mean, it was definitely an elevation. I mean, getting down on the mic with Cube, Mack 10, I mean, heavy hitters. It was like Mack said, it was definitely like a challenge. You couldn't come to the plate unless you was banging off a part and that's what we all trying to do. So I'm happy with the outcome.*

Cube, this is I guess as far as — with concern about your third crew. We all remember N.W.A, Da Lench Mob. What's going to make Westside stick, you know what I'm saying? It's like what's different about it and what's —

Ice Cube: *It ain't nothing different about it. We are individuals, you know? I mean, we're in the Westside Connection but we all in — we stand as individuals. Anything that you hear me saying in a record, I said. Anything that Mack said, Mack said. Anything that Dub said, he said, you know? I mean, we ain't a group like — a group that sit in the garage all day trying to put together things. This is just a collaboration* *that we just felt that we got so much love for each other that it was just — it was good for us and good for the music. That's why we put this album together. Will there be a lot? Will there be one every year? I don't knw, but you never know.*

Thomas: Hip-Hop 2000 TV

First of all, I wanted to give props to the Westside Connection, you know what I'm saying? To Mack 10, W.C. But what I want to know is when the movie coming out?

Ice Cube: What movie [Laughing]. You the second person who asked about a movie. I don't know, man.

Thomas: Hip-Hop 2000 TV

Ain't no parting in the sea because I know it's definitely growing and growing and multiplying and dividing, so I know sooner or later that it's got to be inevitable.

Ice Cube: There's nothing scheduled right now. We just trying to get this record out and just let everybody know what we doing right now, what we into and what we're talking about. So, there ain't a movie in line. Hopefully we'll talk to some people and get one cracking.

Thomas: Hip-Hop 2000 TV

I know "Bow Down" is in heavy rotation all across the nation and everything looks so proper on there, you know what I'm saying? The movie looks like just the next step.

Ice Cube: I hope so.

Are you worried about, like you mentioned Dolores Tucker earlier, are you at all worried about people going to say, "Damn, they make a lot of references to bitches and hoes. They got to get dealt with on this album too, right?"

Ice Cube: It really don't matter what Dolores Tucker, or whoever, because they can't stop it, you know? It's people talking to people. That's what records are: entertainment. Everybody loves the shit we doing. It ain't no mystery. Everybody who really, really, really, really have a problem with the word "bitch" and the word "ho" really don't have a problem with it because they either use it in they daily lives, they listen to it, they watch it on TV and they deal with that word in their community all day every day. They got to expect that if we doing the kind of record that we doing, we're going to deal with it until the word leaves the community. So, for some reason or somehow people ain't talking to each other that way, regardless what's a bad word and what's a good word, when people stop talking to each other that way, then the music that mirror the people will stop dealing with them words and dealing with them terms.

Mack 10, you from Inglewood and W.C. and Cube in South Central mostly. How do you keep your lyrics real to where you ain't like dissing people from South Central or...

Mack 10: *Because I really don't even give a fuck. I ain't into that as far as trying to gang bang and shit and worried about Dub and them wearing blue and Cube wearing blue. I just rap from the heart, homeboy. Whatever I say that's — Fuck it! But it's like I wasn't on that vibe anyway as far as disrespecting, so I didn't even think about none of that shit. I get along with everybody. I'm just like a worldwide kind of dude, you know what I'm saying? I get along with everybody. If we can get some money, I don't care if you from the red side or the blue side, I'm on the green side. I want some money. But yeah, I grew up around Bloods but I don't trip off it. I can't help where my mama lived, so it's all good with us.*

I know you still cool with Dre and all that. What happened to that collaboration? You guys were going to be doing good. And what do you think about Tupac always throwing up the W?

Ice Cube: *I love it! I love it! I mean, we need to show some true California love, you know what I'm saying? Some true California love worldwide.*

And the real question is will these cats unite and do something together.

Ice Cube: Of course, of course because we are businessmen and we know how to work together and not bump heads and still advance in the game that we in. Dre record didn't work because I was doing a lot of things, he was doing a lot of things and it just never came together. We was just too busy to really even know what we was talking about. He know, but it might happen in the future. I hope so.

Mark Sneed: Roots Magazine

My question is you just said that you all are businessmen. Well, I know that a majority of artists make a lot of money touring. How far can Westside Connection go? Is it only gonna be a west of the Mississippi tour 'cause once you get to the other side I assume you will have a bit of tension coming from there.

Ice Cube: No tension at all. No tension, not at all. We ain't got no problem nowhere.

Mack 10.: And we'll still make money.

Ice Cube: We got people booking us all up and down the east coast. They want to, so they wouldn't do it if they didn't think people was going to come in the building.

Michael: Hip-Hop 2000 TV

Cube said something earlier about — basically what he was saying was not selling out to sell records. Personally, I'd like to thank him for that because we got a young kid, like my kid right here. As role models we don't want them thinking that you got to sell out just to get over, you know what I'm saying. Basically, I want to say peace to Westside Connection for keeping it real.

Ice Cube: That's real. Yeah, well, we say what's on our mind, you know. That's just it. We just say what's on our mind, we put it on wax. If it sell, we happy. If it don't we mad. That's just how it is.

Do you think the general public and the press takes what rappers have to say too seriously?

Ice Cube: No, I think they should take what we say very seriously because it's something said from the heart unlike other kind of music where it's cool for somebody else to write your song and shit. It ain't cool for that in Hip-Hop. Somebody find out that you didn't write that dope ass rhyme, they know it didn't come from your soul, from your heart and they shit on you. But everything we say is true. I mean, you know. You should take what we say very seriously. Of course, I mean, just listen. If people listen, they can differentiate the bullshit from what's real and kids are very smart, man. People underestimate kids and what they know and what the fuck they know of. They know more about this shit then we do. They know who said what, when, this, that, and the other.

What I'm saying is like — so, someone on the east coast they're going to say, "Oh, he's dissing Ice Cube." And get into fights about it and discuss it like it's a biblical rule or something like that, you know what I mean?

Ice Cube: What we talking about is real issues. You know, like fucking welfare and the tax cut to the Hip-Hop nation. What we talking about is real to the heart issues. They live for the music, they love the music. Hell yeah, you — same with — people will fucking fight over a Football game. You know you shouldn't be taking that shit serious at all. It's a game, but what we're talking about is — it affects people and a lot of people are thinking how we think, they just scared to say it, but they want to say it.

Is this it for the Westside Connection? Or are you looking to expand and bring more brothers in that are on the west coast as well as the east coast to do albums together?

Ice Cube: Well, we trying to create a worldwide Westside, so we going to bring people in, real picky. Real, real picky now.

Fuck all the critics in the N-Y-C
And your articles tryin to rate my LP
Fuck your backpacks and your wack ass raps
Sayin we ain't real because we make snaps
Sellin six-fos to the Japs, what you lookin at?
With your Brooklyn hat and your pen and pad,
nigga
I got a pocket full of green busting at the seams
Fuck your baggy jeans, fuck your magazines

Ice Cube – *"All The Critics In New York"*

photo by Harris Rosen
Westside Connection BOW DOWN press conference Priority Records HQ
Summer 1996 Hollywood, Ca

CHAPTER 8
WESTSIDE CONNECTION VS NEW YORK CITY MEDIA

When Westside Connection banded together, the intention and main goal of Ice Cube, W.C. and Mack 10, which carried over to the Bow Down album, was to make a dynamic statement by breaking down barriers set in place by New York City based media, radio, and video shows in order to create a unified worldwide Westside.

There were a legion of artists and groups based on the west coast releasing independent albums and setting up distribution networks of their own, who had gone virtually ignored by east coast based media. Fueled by competition and an even stronger desire to get paid, many of these releases achieved sales in the hundreds of thousands, solely relying on hard work, word of mouth, and help of savvy retailers and distributors across California and the southern states. These are the artists and movement for whom Westside Connection put down a strong case.

Demanding the same respect, media coverage, and airplay as New York City based artists, Westside Connection stood for one banded together Westside to proudly flaunt their gangster roots and throw up the W as one.

This whole East/West thing I know earlier in the day it was like a big beef and then we tried to squash it. Where we at with it now?

Ice Cube: I don't know, I really don't. I just know what I know and what I think and how I feel, you know? And I choose to make that public and put it on a record. We all do the same thing. Is it good for Hip-Hop? Yeah, because this shit got to stop. "Westside Slaughterhouse" was really — the reason we did that record because Masta Ace did a record called "Slaughtahouse" where he was kind of mocking the type of shit we do, the form of Hip-Hop we do. That's how "Westside Slaughterhouse" had evolved. Now, I hope everybody ain't looking at Westside Connection as, "Oh, y'all egging this on. Y'all fueling the fire." Because the shit still ain't out. We still ain't getting our records played like we playing records. We play everybody, man. We bump everybody, you know what I'm saying?

Masta Ace - "Slaughtahouse" (https://youtu.be/dQ120j3quJU)

Mack 10: When I was in New York, you don't hear no west coast music, not unless an east coast artist rapping on the song with him or something.

Ice Cube: And that's terrible because that's the — I mean, y'all got to understand that we respect that as the mecca of Hip-Hop, and it should be right there because if it ain't right there, it ain't going to be right anywhere else. But when you start dealing with the politics of Rap, you start dealing with press, you start dealing with video shows. All the video shows on the east coast, you know what I'm saying? If we allow their artists to shit on us, pretty soon these people are going to start shitting on us and they ain't going to start playing our music in rotation at all like we ain't getting played at radio like we should. So we can't allow that to go on, so it stops right here with us. And you know how we feel, we ain't holding no grudges. We ain't holding no grudges at all. We just who we are and that's just it.

W.C.: A lot of people, they try to paint a picture to where we just all out east coast killas. I mean, we cool with some artists on the east coast.

Some artists on the east coast is cool with us. Real recognize real, worldwide, that's how I feel. As far wise as me just seeing someone from the east coast and just taking off on 'em and trippin', that's bullshit.

Ice Cube: *We hate New York critics because they keep a lot of bullshit in the game.*

W.C.: *Exactly.*

Ice Cube: *When they should — they really have the power to unify but they don't. So, that's what we into.*

You said a couple years ago that moving to — going to New York to do Amerikkka's Most was like the best move you've made. So I want to know if you still felt that way and if you don't, what is the best move you've made now.

Ice Cube: *I still work with Producers from the east coast. Going to New York was the perfect move for me at that time. I couldn't get the dopest producer on the west, so I went for the dopest ones on the east, which was the Bomb Squad. I ain't got no problem working with no New York Producers at all. I don't feel no different than I felt. I feel that it's a lot of bullshit in the game that needs to be ironed out in '96, '97, however long it take to really — for people everywhere to respect music from everywhere because it's going to be wack and there's going to be dope from everywhere. We accept all dope-ness from everywhere and we reject all wackness but it ain't like that. We got some dope records that don't get no love. Where everything, the magazines, newspapers, everything mostly come out of New York that really gets our record sales going, big publications, and we just can't have it. If it's going to be a war, it's just going to be all out.*

What do you have to say to critics and the media who say that this East/West coast beef was really being perpetuated by record artists labels so they can sell more units and that the average Joe doesn't have anything to do with it.

Mack 10: *They don't really know what they talking about.*

Ice Cube: Yeah, I'm in the business to sell units, but I've never bit my tongue so I could sell records because I'm gonna to sell records. I got enough fans to sell records whatever I want to say, you know? If we wanted to sell records we could just do some more happy, cool songs. I mean, we could do a Hip-Hop song that's radio friendly and all that. We can do anything that we need to do to sell records, you know what I'm saying? But we want to sell records, but we also want to say what needs to be said. I look at Hip-Hop not just as music and entertainment and this, that, and the other, but more of like a history of what these kids and what we going through from the early '80s all the way until now. Anytime you want to know what was going on in '83, you go buy the records from that era and you'll know what the people feel. In '96, Westside Connection, that's how we feel. It may be different in '97, but I doubt it.

I know you said that you're not getting music played on the east coast. Is it also jumping into the line of you being able to do shows on the east coast as well? Are they responding to you on that?

Ice Cube: I never had a problem. I never had a problem with either getting love on the east coast or whatever. That ain't really the point I'm trying to convey. What I'm trying to say is that there is a problem with other artists, you know what I'm saying? Not just from the west coast, from the south, from the southeast, other artists who getting shitted on, and that's what this is about. It ain't about me particularly getting 100,000 record sales in New York or nothing like that. It's just me saying, "Well shit, man. Just respect the music. Fuck where we from. That shouldn't even be in it. Listen to the music, respecting if it's dope enough play it on your station."

So, like I said, it's like Washington, DC not listening to fuckin' California. That's what it feels like in Hip-Hop right now, you know? Now everybody's, "Oh, there ain't no problem." "Ain't no problem? What y'all talking about?" "Nah, nah. People are tripping. Y'all tripping." We ain't tripping. This shit has evolved into what it is now so we should deal with it right now and hopefully we'll be through with it.

So I guess what I'm hearing is that you're calling — you're speaking out because you're widely listened to across the country and you're saying, "Let's put a stop to this," primarily.

Ice Cube: I'm saying here's how we feel. It ain't up to me to put a stop to it. And I ain't really — whatever the people are going to do, people are going to do, but this is how we feel about it on the west coast. By you seeing all these people throwing up the W, everybody won't say it, but they feel the same way and they show unity and they show they down with what we saying when they throw up the W. That's what I see.

What kind of response have you guys been receiving 'cause basically for a year you've been releasing songs and you've been hitting hard on this topic. And have you changed any attitudes with any people in the press that you were having problems from or other artists? Or what kind of feedback have you been getting?

Ice Cube: I don't know. I mean, I've seen people in the press during these last couple of months, or this last, or, whatever, who were first keeping this thing going as far as east... really New York turning nose down on everything else. They was keeping that going with they little articles and now they want to stop the problem. They want to really — it seem like the press has really changed their attitude and they're trying to stop the problem. Maybe it'll fizz out and maybe it won't. That don't mean we don't feel like we feel when we ain't going to say it. I mean, we'll be who we are because we really don't care about — I mean, the press keep a lot of shit in the game and that's just true because people — They can't call me on the phone and talk to me so they got to read your articles, or they got to see us on soundbites and this, that, and the other. They keep a lot of shit in the game, but that's the press job, shit, to sell whatever they trying to sell and to keep shit in the game.

What about other artists? I mean, are other artists coming to you saying, "I'm glad you guys did..."

Ice Cube: Every artist east and west don't want no problems, that's what I'm getting from the artists. But it's said now, but it wasn't said in '94, '93, when the east surge was coming back and then it was not only an east surge again, but it was shitting on the west with that surge, you know what I'm saying? That ain't good.

Y'all know me, still the same O.G. but I been low-
key
Hated on by most these niggas with no cheese
No deals and no G's
No wheels and no keys, no boats, no snowmobiles,
and no skis
Mad at me cause I can finally afford to provide my
family with groceries
Got a crib with a studio and it's all full of tracks
To add to the wall full of plaques
Hanging up in the office in back of my house like
trophies
Did y'all think I'ma let my dough freeze, ho please
You better bow down on both knees
Who you think taught you to smoke trees
Who you think brought you the oldies
Eazy-E's, Ice Cubes, and D.O.C's
The Snoop D-O-double-G's
And the group that said motha fuck the police
Gave you a tape full of dope beats
To bump when you stroll through in your hood
And when your album sales wasn't doing too good
Who's the Doctor they told you to go see
Y'all better listen up closely
All you niggas that said that I turned pop
Or The Firm flopped
Y'all are the reason that Dre ain't been getting no
sleep
So fuck y'all, all of y'all
If y'all don't like me, blow me
Y'all are gonna keep fucking around with me and
turn me back to the old me

Dr. Dre – *"Forgot About Dre"*

photo by Harris Rosen
B-Real at Muggs Presents The Soul Assassins release party March 1997
Hollywood, Ca

CHAPTER 9
ICE CUBE VS CYPRESS HILL

There are three sides to every story. Your side. My side. And the truth. In 1996, long-time friends Ice Cube and Cypress Hill went to war for an entire year.

In the 1996 press conference at Priority Records HQ, Ice Cube was asked to comment on the hard hitting Westside Connection diss song, "King of the Hill", where he and Mack 10 lashed out at Cypress Hill.

Westside Connection - "King of the Hill"
(https://youtu.be/SX7KsU9MwEo)

Months before the release of the Bow Down album and "King of the Hill", B-Real visited Toronto on a promotional trip for Cypress Hill III: Temples of Boom. In an exclusive interview, he spoke in detail on what led up to the war with Ice Cube and his strong feelings in regards to the matter.

To the delight of millions, Dr. Dre and Ice Cube had reconciled in 1994 and recorded the hard hitting "Natural Born Killaz" for Death Row Records Murder Was the Case soundtrack. Dre was also friends with B-Real. During our exclusive November 1996 interview he commented on the beef between Ice Cube and B-Real.

Dr. Dre & Ice Cube - "Natural Born Killaz"
(https://youtu.be/w8sDp65dyeA)

Muggs is a founding member of Cypress Hill, Producer, DJ, and core member of the Soul Assassins art collective with Mister Cartoon and Estevan Oriol. In January 1997, he was preparing for the March release of Muggs presents The Soul Assassins, Chapter 1. His debut solo album featured "Puppet Master" with both Dr. Dre and B-Real and a top shelf selection of elite east, west and south artists, including RZA & GZA, GooDie Mob, KRS-One, MC Eiht, Mobb Deep, and Wyclef. During our exclusive interview at his downtown Los Angeles Soul Assassins HQ, he relayed his side of the story, provided a shocking update and filled us in on where he stood with Ice Cube at the time.

Soul Assassins featuring Dr. Dre & B-Real - "Puppet Master"
(https://youtu.be/Ht4H4nW8cUI)

Ice Cube: Well, Cypress Hill... It goes back to — they did a song for me on the Friday soundtrack, and I went to the studio to get the song. Now, they did the last song on the soundtrack. We were waiting for them. I went to the studio personally to get the DAT from them. Well, they had played me a couple other DAT's when they was there — you know, when I was there, but I had my song finished and they had a couple songs and we was kind of like half-assed listening to them and half-assed talking. I do my song, my song come out and like three months later I go to South Africa to do my movie and Mack 10 called me and say, "Cypress Hill is on the radio dissing you." I said, "What?!" And I didn't understand it, so I called B-Real and it was a misunderstanding where they thought that I took one of they hooks, and this, that, and the other.

So everything was supposed to be squashed. Well, a couple of weeks later, evidently, they couldn't squash it or they didn't want to squash it so they had did records and they was dissing and all this, that, and the other. So, you know me, I don't run from no challenge from nobody. Even though we was dogs, I felt like they should be dealt with the worst because we were friends, you know what I'm saying? That's why we got the attitude like Westside Connection and really like fuck everybody who really ain't really — who in our way. We ain't trying to fuck with nobody just to do it, but if they in our way, that's how we coming. Cypress Hill was one of those and "King of the Hill" is how we had to deal with it.

B-Real: *It's a pretty long story but I'll try and break it down as quick as I can for you. We were doing a song for the Friday soundtrack. Somewhere around the line on tour he told us about the movie way before they started on it and he said if we wanted to do the shit. He said, "Fuck yeah!" I was even supposed to be in the movie but there was confusion in the management we had so I didn't get to do it. But we made up for it by doing the song, which is "Roll It Up, Light It Up (Smoke It Up)". And when we had finished the song we called him down to the studio to hear it and make sure that that's what he wanted, and he liked it. He says, "Yeah, man, that's cool." We said, "Hey, yo, we got a few songs here from our album, you want to check them out?" He says, "Oh, hell yeah!" We played him five songs. One of 'em was "Throw Your Set In The Air" and he really liked that. He was like "Yo, that's the shit, man! Play that shit again." So he played it again and then he asked us "Hey, man. Can I have that for the soundtrack?" We're like well normally we would give it to you, man, but this is gonna be our single and we're dead set on this being our single, so we'll let you have anything else. He says, "Nah, that's cool. I wanted that one but fuck it I'll just take the "Roll It Up, Light It Up" then."*

Right before we go on Lollapalooza, I hear a song on the radio and a piece of "Throw Your Set" was on "Friday", which was 'Oh yeah, throw your neighbourhood in the air like you don't care', which is twisted around from 'Throw Your Set In The Air, wave it around like you just don't care' 'cause set and neighbourhood are the same thing. So knowing that, I was like, okay, fuck it. I'm a let it slide. I come back from Lollapalooza and I hear another bite, which is on Kausion's album, 'cause I had did something for Kausion for Cube right before we left on Lollapalooza, even though I knew he bit, and I already know, but I still treated him like a friend. Came back and I heard a piece from "Throw

Your Set In The Air" was the title of Kausion's album. So, he took that piece and titled it and then used it in a song.

Cypress Hill - "Throw Your Set In The Air"
(https://youtu.be/TMRbDF-Ea8M)

Ice Cube - "Friday"
(https://youtu.be/IPw9gbbQ1xA)

I was like, fuck, he just all the way fucked me and he didn't give a fuck. So, I kept thinking about it. I said, well, you know what, fuck this! We were friends and if he really considered me a friend he wouldn't have stole the shit the way he did. He could have asked me for it. Then he calls me from South Africa denying the shit. "Yo, yo, I, I, I, I, I heard you guys were talking shit. Yo man, we're homeboys, man. Yo, what's up?" And I told him, "Hey man, we let you hear some shit and now its on your song, what's up?" "Um Um Um Um I, I, I had a verse, man." You know, just stuttering and I knew that he was stuttering he was lying because Cube will never stutter if he's telling you some straight shit. You know, if y'all ever did an interview with him when he's talking to you he's solid. There's no stuttering. If a man is solid, every time a man is lying and you can tell is when he's stuttering 'cause he's thinking of what he's gonna say next. So I said, alright Cube, it's cool, whatever, and we let the shit fly for a while.

Then I just got mad. I said, fuck, man! I watched his back for so long. I stood up for him when motherfuckers talked shit about him and he's gonna fuck me like I'm nobody! So, I said, fuck it. Let's just do this song. He's playing me like I'm some kind of fool. What does he think that I smoke so much weed that I wouldn't notice, or that I'd just be like passive about it and not let it out. He's got to feel the repercussions. So that's why we made the song. I feel bad because I really considered him a friend. So when I go around saying shit that he done it's fucking with me because I was like, "Fuck yeah! Us and Cube! We're the downest crew in L.A. and we're down together and can't nobody fuck with us" and he went and broke that. I would be more than willing to squash the shit if he would just admit it, you know. But if he don't want to admit it then fuck him and feed him. When I see him on the street I want to see what *he's going to do. Truth is on my side. That's why I'm not worried about what he's gonna say about us. He can't say shit 'cause we never fucked nobody. We're always pretty straight with everybody unless we don't like you.*

He's the type of motherfucker, let me just tell you what he's done. He ripped off King Sun. People have sent demos to him and he'll take the shit off the demos knowing that these groups ain't gonna get no record deal. Knowing that nobody's gonna believe them if they say anything. Knowing that these songs ain't copy-written. He'll put 'em out and what are these motherfuckers gonna say? He chose the wrong group to do that to because we sell as many as him, if not more. We don't need extra controversy. We don't need to go out and diss Cube to sell records and make people buy our shit. We're just telling the truth about his ass and he's trying to switch it all into this racial shit like "Oh, they're mad because Black people don't buy their records no more. They're alternative now." What the fuck does he think he is?! The same people that buy our records are the same people that buys his records. He did Lollapalooza before us. He had the Chili Peppers in his video knowing that they're fucking fags. And he's gonna say shit about us. He can kiss my fucking ass. I mean, when I see him he better be ready. I'm gonna knock his fucking fat ass out. He can take me to court. I'm willing to lose the money 'cause I know we're right.

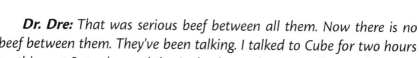

Dr. Dre: *That was serious beef between all them. Now there is no beef between them. They've been talking. I talked to Cube for two hours on this past Saturday and they're back together. Actually, we all plan to ... I just did a song with B-Real called "Puppet Masters" and it'll be out soon. We just did a video together and everything. All three of us plan to sit down in a room and we're gonna go on tour this time next year. We're starting on our albums. Cube's starting on his. Cypress is starting on theirs. I'm starting on mine. All of us are gonna put them together. We're gonna appear on each other's records and we're all going out on*

tour together. Cube talked Friday and they squashed all of their disagreements.

DJ Muggs: *We heard about this shit from all the King Sun. We heard about it from Volume 10. We've heard about it from Chip from the Torcha Chamba, from Kam, from DJ Pooh. You know, Pooh wrote Friday's with Cube, got no credit. A lot of shit. We was like "We don't give a fuck what you do, just don't do it to us."*

It's on now - bam! Did a record about him, all true. He did a record about us, made up all kind of shit. You heard the underground record we did about him? "Ice Cube Killa". I'll get you a copy. We took his beat off the Westside Connection the day after his record came out and put it out on the streets three days later, flipped it on him, tore him a new asshole with his beat. I'll get you a copy of it, might have one in the car. We only bootlegged it. We don't want to release it commercially. We printed up 3000 of them, passed them out. We're printing up another 3000 and we're giving 'em out, givin' it out. We're not even sellin' it!

Kam - Pull Your Hoe Card
(https://www.youtube.com/watch?v=f6VmTmlrZ_A)

DJ Pooh feat. Kam - Whoop Whoop
(https://www.youtube.com/watch?v=3N0AQtkOilE)

Kam Details Squashing His Beef with Ice Cube at Minister Farrakhan's Home
(https://www.youtube.com/watch?v=QTMf-T8jxT8)

Cypress Hill - "Ice Cube Killa"
(https://youtu.be/-SeC-0kRCpY)

So, I guess we've hooked up with Kam. We've been working with Kam a little bit and you know Cube got into a little scrap with Solo (Kam's DJ), got his chain snatched. B-Real was wearing Cube's Westside

Connection chain onstage out here at House of Blues, taking pictures for magazines, flossing with it. Saying, if you man enough to come back and get it come pick it up. Two days later, Cube called B-Real, they talked. I don't know what was said but B-Real told me that he talked to Cube, everything's cool now. We're in the process of making everything be cool.

I'm like, iight, whatever, I still got to holler at him. That's cool. I always liked Cube as an MC. He's been one of my favourite artists all the time. He was even a cool brother but when he's pulling that shit, you know what I mean? He still owes me some money from The Predator album 'cause I did "Check Yo Self". They come around and put the single out. I know they remixed it and everything but I'm still supposed to get production credit. He didn't give it to me, still owe me a little bit of cheddar from that but I'll deal with that when I see him. I heard Kam on the radio with Pooh the other night. Kam's like, "Yeah, we're talking to Cube too." I guess they must have got with Kam and Cube's trying to squash all his shit. I guess every once in a while a man needs to get put in check and realize his mistakes and what's really going on."

photo by Harris Rosen
Westside Connection BOW DOWN press conference Priority Records HQ
Summer 1996 Hollywood, Ca

CHAPTER 10
WESTSIDE CONNECTION VS Q-TIP & COMMON

C ypress Hill is not the only crew Westside Connection railed against on the Bow Down album. Q-Tip and Common also received their share of a lyrical beatdown. Q-Tip went hard at the west coast over a cracking beat on The Classic Collection Doo Wop 95 Live mixtape track "Representin' Queens." *"To you west coast haters we will bust your shit. This is how it is, you get blown plus dick. Check it, I denote that I denounce all ya wack niggas like the squad you better bounce."*

Q-Tip "Representin' Queens" (https://youtu.be/yfoPsIOj50M)

In September 1994, Common Sense (now known as Common) released the metaphor laden attack, "I Used to Love H.E.R.", commentating on the fall of conscious rap and ensuing decline of Hip-Hop with the emergence of the west coast gangster rap revolution. Westside Connection included him on "Westside Slaugterhouse" and Common responded with what is rated as possibly the greatest diss track of all-time, "The Bitch in Yoo", over a smooth Pete Rock beat. The Bow Down album provided Westside Connection a prime opportunity to strike back, again.

Common - "The Bitch In Yoo"
(https://youtu.be/YLV7tMVJ_wY)

W.C.: Like Cube said everybody is accountable for their own action even though we all down with each other. Q-Tip had a mix tape out that I'm quite sure some of you probably heard of. He had a line when he said, "To you west coast niggas we'll bust your shit. Y'all can get the some-some plus the dick. Something, something, something, I'll be right here with everything else. All you wack niggas like to squawk you better bounce." Some shit like that. You know, when I heard it and shit, I damn near choked! I was like, not this bitch right here! You know, out of all people, not Q-Tip. I mean, every time I see him it's open arms and everything, so my brother confronted him and asked him what did he say and he was trying to switch up, say he was saying, "To you west coast haters." We was like, "Don't you got haters on the east coast too? Why is it west coast? Are you trying to ride the wave? What's going on? Are you bombing from the back? Or are you just; what's really going on?"

At the time when we did a song called "Cross 'Em Out and Put A K" everybody — we were saying this is a song we're going to let our nuts hang as usual, but we're just going to let motherfuckers have it who we don't like. And at the time, Q-Tip was on my mind and I mentioned Q-Tip name. It was just — I just mentioned his name. I really didn't let him have it the way we could've went all out and let him have it.

Westside Connection - "Cross 'Em Out and Put AK (Cypress Hill & Q-Tip Diss)" (https://youtu.be/SsoNFJS1qQQ)

Basically, Common Sense got problems. He try to — he done got him some liquid courage and shit and got a cape that came along with the beer, I guess, and went and wrote a rap. He really got problems now because we didn't even really go all out on this bitch ass. I'm not sitting there trying to get real violent or nothing like that. I'm just saying that basically with us, we're all coming from the heart with it. We're trying to make good records but at the same time too, like Cube said, whoever speaks on the Westside Connection got to get dealt with and Q-Tip had to get dealt with.

Ice Cube: Common!? It's funny because when he first came out — I mean, he was doing like hip — real old-school Hip-Hop records with the scratching hook and all that. But what "I Used to Love" — I mean, we all know metaphors, you know? I've been in the game since I was 14 so I know metaphors and dude dissed: he talking about this girl that he was in love with, she's supposed to be Hip-Hop and he's so in love with her, but when she go out here she get fucked up. You know what I'm saying? When she started doing it this way, and she ain't as good as she was and I don't really want to have nothing to do with her. And we felt it was a diss, so — at least I did. I mean, everybody did, but I was the first one with the pen, so that's how that started. He took that and he made a record. I mean, hopefully he can make a lot of money out of this, you know what I'm saying? We dissing him ain't going to put no more money in our pockets, so us dissing him is straight from here 'cause Common — you know; Guppy.

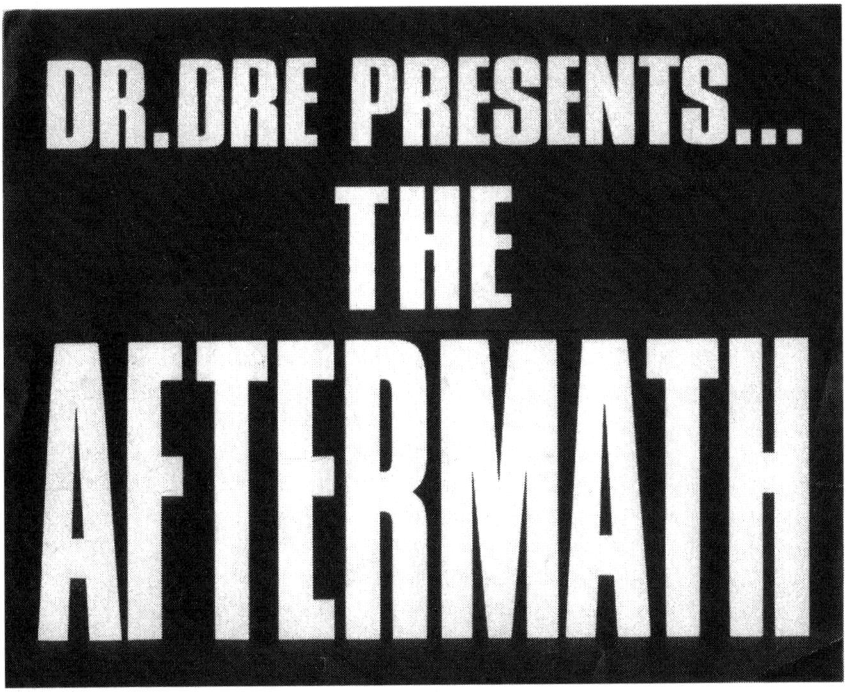
DR.DRE PRESENTS...
THE
AFTERMATH

CHAPTER 11
DR. DRE PRESENTS... THE AFTERMATH

D r. Dre had an incredible run at Death Row Records, manning the boards and producing classic after classic for the label as his stock rose. From the title track to the Deep Cover film and his essential classic The Chronic, to Snoop Doggy Dogg's Doggystyle, Tha Dogg Pound's Dogg Food, various artist film soundtracks Above the Rim and Murder Was the Case, and his work with 2Pac on All Eyez On Me.

During this period Death Row served as a lightning rod for the east coast vs west coast war, and in turn Dr. Dre became caught up in the eye of the storm for better or worse. Tired of the violent undertones and atmosphere permeating the label that had gradually worked their way to being present in his recording sessions, and discontent with what he perceived as a shortfall in his financial rewards, Dr. Dre eventually stopped going to the studio and following a row with violent Death Row Records overlord, Suge Knight, in March 1996, left his half of the company and valuable masters behind.

Suge Knight instantaneously instructed his wards and artists to go into attack mode, and they did. 2Pac led the charge and went in hard. A few of the artists Dr. Dre put on, most notably Daz, joined in too. Disses came fast and furious. There was barely enough time for Dr. Dre to breathe in-between the salvos. He was dodging personal attacks on record, rumours on the streets, and feared for the safety of himself and his family. Though he did manage the time to partner with Jimmy Iovine and Interscope Records to form his own label, Aftermath Entertainment.

Dr. Dre introduced the public-at-large to the arrival of Aftermath Entertainment on November 26, 1996 with Dr. Dre Presents The Aftermath. A compilation of what was to come from the label, the album also included his farewell to Gangster Rap in the form of "Been There, Done That."

This is a rare winter 1996 with Dr. Dre, in the thick of his bitter war with Death Row Records, on the heels of the untimely murder of Tupac Shakur in Las Vegas. Many pictures have been painted and multiple books written concerning this period. It is arguably the most infamous and dark period in modern contemporary music history in which lives were tragically lost. Dr. Dre spoke on his departure from N.W.A and Ruthless Records, Death Row Records, and the beginnings of Aftermath Entertainment, and laid out future plans. He went in on Snoop Doggy Dogg's Tha Doggfather and responded to personal rumours.

Obviously it was a big step leaving Death Row and starting your own label. When did you first start thinking about it?

Dr. Dre: *I can tell you the exact time actually, mid-February 1995.*

You wanted to start Aftermath then?

Dr. Dre: *Yeah, most def.*

But you still stayed down with Death Row?

Dr. Dre: *Yeah, I had to actually wait for the right opportunity and make sure all my shit was together because it was going to be a long time before I was heard again. So, I did the song "California Love" with Tupac and that gave me a little bit of time, that gave me a couple of* *months, while I was getting things together over here. I had to make sure all my shit was together before I bounced.*

How does it feel? Everybody is up in your business. Everybody wants to know what you are doing. Everybody thinks they know what you are doing. They're even questioning your sexuality at times.

Dr. Dre: *Hahahhahaha, that's funny. You know what? None of that shit matters to me. What anybody wants to know. What anybody thinks. What anybody says. It means less than zero to me, you know what I'm sayin'? Because its like this, I've done more shit in my life right now then most people will do in their whole fuckin' lifetime. Until a person is doing what I'm doing, or have accomplished everything that I have accomplished, they have nothing to say to me, absolutely nothing. Seriously. As far as the other shit goes, I'll use one of Mike Tyson's words, that's the most ludicrous shit I ever heard in my life. Straight up, ask my wife.*

This albums seems to be leaning towards R&B. Are you saying in-between the lines Hip-Hop is for kids. I'm losing my love for Hip-Hop. All this gangsterism shit is helping me lose it and just getting into more mature moods and not wanting to deal with all the nonsense.

Dr. Dre: *No. I got a lot of hardcore shit coming up. That just happened to be what came out at that time. The Aftermath LP that's out right now is simply a teaser. You know how you get sampler tapes in the mail of somebody's album? They give you little snippets of what's to come. That's basically what the Aftermath LP is. It's like everybody didn't even put their best cuts on there. I didn't put my best cut on there. "Been There Done That" is like okay. The shit works, it ain't wack but it's workin'. When I did the little video and what have you, and it's working for me. I love hardcore Hip-Hop and that's what I'm gonna continue to do. The lyrical content of it is gonna be a lot different. I'm gonna be positive vibe now but that's it for me. I'm still into it.*

Personally, I can't wait for the King Tee album.

Dr. Dre: *He's in the studio right now. He's in there with Too $hort. They're doing a cut together.*

In the early days you were preyed upon by Eazy-E. It's been documented. Then it seems you were preyed upon by Suge Knight. How are you running your business? What is that causing you to do with your stuff?

Dr. Dre: *Actually, at the beginning I wasn't running my business. I'm a young kid out of Compton. The only thing I was interested in is making Hip-Hop music. That's all. I had some people doing my business which is a very big mistake, which was a very big mistake and I got jerked, straight up. To be perfectly honest, I was getting two points for my production and a motherfucker could come off the street and get four. This is after I had made a couple of platinum records and I went to Eazy with an ultimatum. "Get rid of the fucking manager, Jerry Heller, or I'm leaving. Take a pick". He chose to stay with Jerry Heller and I bounced, went to Death Row.*

Now the Death Row whole incident is like this. I'm not comfortable. I wasn't comfortable and it was time for me to bounce, and it wasn't just one thing. It was an accumulation of things. You got motherfuckers getting beat down for no reason, Engineers and shit like that, and I ain't with that. I want to get down and make some music. I ain't trying to be no mother-fucking gangster or fighting and all that. I want to make some music and have fun and party. I'm a fighter, not... I mean, I'm a lover not a fighter. Fuck all that! It was just; I can give you an example and I've said this before, if you're at a party and you go to this party and there is some people there that don't have your best interest in mind, or you not comfortable with those people being there you're gonna leave the party and you gonna go home. Well, now I feel like I'm at home with the Aftermath.

Death Row's Chief Engineer Interview Part 1: Suge Knight, Dre Leaving Death Row & The Makaveli Album (https://youtu.be/udeCub17sGI)

How are you treating your artists? Are you giving them a fair shake? Are they signed to you? How is that structured?

Dr. Dre: *My artists are definitely getting a fair shake. I do not deal with anybody unless they have an attorney and the attorney works out the deal. I make sure that the artist understands everything that's in the contract before they sign, straight up. They have to know everything that they're getting into because it's their life. It's your life. It's a twenty-four hour job, straight up. They have to know the whole shit.*

It isn't called the music business for nothing.

Dr. Dre: *Right. It's the record business. There is two words there. You make records and you handle your business, straight up.*

Going back to what you were saying and slap-outs in the studio and all that. I have a friend, who shall remain nameless, who was there when Suge Knight personally slapped out DeVante because he didn't give him his drum sound on a tape.

Dr. Dre: *Oh, no shit.*

And certain guys hanging around him for specific reasons.

Dr. Dre: *Yeah, I ain't gonna get into all that shit but the shit just wasn't cool, straight up. It wasn't just, damn, you know. Shit wasn't --- The whole atmosphere was like, it was like going to work. When you making Hip-Hop music its not supposed to be like work. It's supposed to be fun, man. Although it is work, it is work. It can be hectic but it's supposed to -- Your environment is not supposed to be like fucked up like that. People coming in and partying and you know, put some beats down and that's that. You don't need all the other drama. I ain't mad at nobody.*

Would you say you weren't doing east coast music. You weren't really caring what they were doing and you were totally on a west coast vibe, your own vibe.

Dr. Dre: *That's totally false. That's totally false. I've always loved east coast music. I love east coast music now. I've always loved west coast music. I don't consider my music to be labelled as no fucking, no city's music. This is Dre's music. It's not no west coast music. It's not no west coast sound. Its not no east coast music, no east sound. No southern, no northern, no nothing. This is Dre's sound, period. A lot of people say my shit sounds like east coast music. Some people say it sounds like west coast music. What is that? It's just, okay, tell me what's the difference between east coast and west coast music? You can't. There is no difference except they talk different. We talk different. That's all it is to it. Their shit might sound a little dirtier, or whatever, but it doesn't matter. I can do a track for you and I'm born and raised on the west coast and play it for you and tell you what east coast person did it and you would believe me. You wouldn't be able to just say and put a label on it and say, "No! That shit came from the west coast." There is no way you would be able to do that.*

You're tight with Ice Cube. If you and Ice Cube are tight and he's upset with you working with Cypress, you do what you do, but what I'm getting at is are all these Rappers creating games and beefs and all that to punch up to the press and laughing at people from their mountain homes? Or, is it all real?

Dr. Dre: *No. That was serious beef between them. Now there is no beef between them. They've been talking. I talked to Cube for two hours on this past Saturday and they're back together. Actually, we all plan to; I just did a song with B-Real called "Puppet Masters" and it'll be out soon. We just did a video together and everything. All three of us plan to sit down in a room and we're gonna go on tour this time next year. We're starting on our albums. Cube's starting on his. Cypress is starting on theirs. I'm starting on mine. All of us is gonna put them together. We're gonna appear on each other's records and we're all going out on tour together. Cube talked Friday and they squashed all of their disagreements.*

Do you still value your street rep?

Dr. Dre: *Um, what's that? What do you mean by that?*

Do you still care what the kids on the streets say, or you just look in the mirror and you're happy.

Dr. Dre: *I'm trying to understand more about what you're saying. Do I care what the kids say about me?*

About your music, about where your head is, about your sound and the way it's transforming.

Dr. Dre: *Well, yes I care, then I don't care. I care about if people are digging my music or not because once you do a record you want somebody to dig it. There's nothing saying that they're going too but I do want kids to like my shit. I want everybody to like my shit. I'm not singling out kids in the ghetto. I want everybody to like my music. Its not always guaranteed that everybody's going to like it, and as far as Dr. ... as far as Andre Young goes, it's like I don't give a fuck what anybody thinks about me. I'm going to do what I want to do when I want to do it, straight up. I don't give a fuck what anybody thinks about me because I'm cool. I'm straight. I'm chillin'.*

Hip-Hop dominates the pop charts now. Would you say its pop music, or would you say its still a culture?

Dr. Dre: *Definitely still a culture. It's a culture that has happened to have gotten popular.*

What do you think of Snoop's album, Tha Doggfather? Obviously you've heard it, when he says we don't need Dre and he just cracks any old beat up and rhymes over it. Did you take that as an insult?

Dr. Dre: *Actually, no, I don't think its an insult. I think he played hisself by saying that. Snoop is my boy. That's like my little brother, straight up, but he played his-self for saying that because he said that and then this corny ass beat comes on. It sounds like a track that I would have threw away.*

Snoop Doggy Dogg - "Freestyle Conversation" (https://youtu.be/l_3oeY18nm4)

To me, that was the point of the song.

Dr. Dre: *I have no idea. I never listened to the whole song. I haven't listened to the whole album. I don't really like the album but I think its getting a bad rap because he went in, he put a lot of work into it. He had a lot of weight riding on his shoulders coming off a classic album. Doggystyle was a big record. Doggystyle is a classic Hip-Hop album. Coming off of that without having the Producer that brung him into the game, working with new Producers and trying to produce himself, on his most important record. Tha Doggfather was much more important than Doggystyle, by far, because this is like everybody was waiting and watching to see what he was going to do, so he has a lot of weight on his shoulders. It's not a wack album but it's not a good one either.*

Something tells me that you had tracks ready for that album. Either never handed them in or they got scrapped when the split happened.

Dr. Dre: *For Doggfather? Yeah, most definitely did. You'll be hearing them soon. On something else. I have some bomb tracks, some real dope tracks. The worst tracks is better than the best one on that record.*

Hopefully King Tee is hitting those songs. I can't wait for that album.

Dr. Dre: *He has a fucking smash album, man. He has until June and he has like about, I think, nine songs and all of 'em are bangin'. But we gonna go through about 40 songs and then just pick out the best 14.*

Now that Tupac is gone and Suge Knight is on lockdown, have you thought about working or approaching Death Row artists and restructuring and not acting as barbarians and doing this for the love of music only?

Dr. Dre: *Why would I do that? No! I mean, as far as I'm concerned right now Death Row doesn't even exist. I don't do backflips. I'm looking* *for the future. My eyes are on tomorrow not yesterday, straight up. I would love to work with Snoop. I would love to work with Kurupt. I would love to work with Rage. I would love to work with Nate Dogg. Those are the four artists that I really got love for from Death Row. Everybody else, I can't do nothing for ya, man. It's gonna happen. Me and Snoop are gonna work together in the future. Those four artists I just named to you, we'll be working together at some time in the future. When, I don't know.*

I heard Kurupt moved back to Philly.

Dr. Dre: *I don't know. It doesn't matter. Those four artists I just named we will work together again. If it's fuckin' ten years from now.*

A friend who lives in Los Angeles told me that Daz was on 92.3 The Beat saying that you've been taking credit for his beats.

Dr. Dre: *That shit is fucking crazy! Daz could not fucking sit in the same room with me and say that I took anything. I never put my name on jack shit that I didn't do, straight up. I ain't no fuckin' Milli Vanilli! I don't put my name on shit I don't do.*

What would he have to gain by saying that?

Dr. Dre: *I don't know. What they're trying to do is to make the public not like me anymore because I left them. Daz couldn't fucking see me with binoculars, straight up, in the studio. I taught him how to work a fucking drum machine. Why the fuck would I want one of his beats? Straight up. And I'll tell him that shit to his face! He's a lying motherfucker!*

Why is all this going on? In the past it appeared you had nothing but love for each other. Why is all the bullshit happening? Is it because of the green?

Dr. Dre: *The same reason why it happened; the same reason why it happened with Tupac. I mean, very, very, well, very easily influenced. I left Death Row. Now everybody there is mad at me. So, "Okay, fuck Dre! Let's talk some shit about him!" For one, Tupac did a whole song dissing* me, right. One, Tupac never knew me. He never knew me! Tupac had never been to my house before. He doesn't even know where I live. We never even been in the same car together. The only thing we did was went in the studio together, made a song, went to the video shoot, did the video. That's it. So, how can he fucking diss me saying anything about me?! That's all fucking hype. That's hype! Straight up.

Junior High behavior.

Dr. Dre: *That shit is so fucking childish, man. You exactly right. That shit is childish. That's why I don't even respond to shit, man. It's like, 'Okay, what's next?' If that's how you feel. If you're a fucking man that's what you should have said to me. Not on a fucking record! If you got a problem with me. Fuck! So that's that.*

I guess that's part of the reason you released "Been There, Done That". It's sort of a closure.

Dr. Dre: *Most definitely. That's it. I didn't really even like the song. Everybody digs it so I put it on the fuckin' record. It's like okay, the shit works. I got some much flyer shit. I got some serious shit finna to come out. I'm doing the American Pimp soundtrack; the Hughes Brothers documentary on Pimps. And I have a song I'm doing called "Black People" and I'm also doing a song called "Dre Day Part 2". There's gonna be some wicked shit.*

Dr. Dre - "Been There, Done That"
(https://youtu.be/c80dWbiONqM)

Have you signed or approached other artists to work with Aftermath? I heard a rumour you were trying to speak with the Fu-Schnickens.

Dr. Dre: *Yeah, they'll be signing. Definitely.*

Any other surprises?

Dr. Dre: *Hopefully I'll be doing some work with Rakim. We'll see* *how that goes. That's not a definite yet. Maybe some work with Erykah Badu. Badoo, Badu, I can't remember how to fuckin say it. I'm going to see her tonight at the Billboard club out here, she's playing. She said she wanted to meet me and shit. So, I haven't met her or nothing but everybody's talking about me and her working together and that's something that I would like to do. She's the shit.*

What's coming up for Aftermath?

Dr. Dre: *Soundtracks. Films. Albums.*

When?

Dr. Dre: *About three albums out this year.*

One thing I got to say about this Aftermath album is that the packaging is over the top.

Dr. Dre: *Hahahaha, that's some wild shit, eh.*

I still can't get with Mel-Man.

Dr. Dre: *That's wild, hahaha. Mel-Man is fucking crazy. He's a comedian. He just don't give a fuck. He's not even a Rapper, man. He's a Producer. He just wanted to do that. Like I said, man. Everybody on this record is like, "Okay, let me do a song" and we did it, okay. And the shit is selling like a motherfucker, so that's cool. But the best is yet to come.*

photo by Harris Rosen
DJ Yella February 20, 2014 DRE DAY Toronto, Canada

CHAPTER 12
FRIENDS?

N.W.A went through multiple life-changing experiences together in the studio and on tour. Adored by millions, yet persecuted by the authorities and moral majority anywhere and everywhere they laid their caps, N.W.A was under constant surveillance by the F.B.I., L.A.P.D., and every Police force nationwide. Though short-lived as a group, they had banded together as one to fight the power and "Fuck the Police." But did they develop an undying bond?

Dr. Dre and Yella had come up together as local club DJs and members of the World Class Wreckin' Cru. Ice Cube was a member of C.I.A. with Dre's cousin Sir Jinx and they often performed together at various parties Dre hosted. Dre even connected Cube with World Class Wreckin' Cru where he contributed lyrics to their 1987 club hit "Cabbage Patch".

World Class Wreckin' Cru - "Cabbage Patch"
(https://youtu.be/g09hEdZAe4M)

MC Ren had signed with Ruthless Records as a High-School student and wrote a significant amount of lyrics for Eazy-E to deliver on the Eazy-Duz-It album before being invited to join the group.

Yella spoke on the status of his relationships with Dr. Dre, Ice Cube and Ren in the exclusive 1996 interview. Jerry Heller had Dr. Dre on his mind during the exclusive 2006 interview.

Yella: *When I talked to Dre for the first time last week I told him I'm glad he's on his success. I'm glad he did good. I tell Cube and Ren, all of them the same. I ain't jealous of nobody. That's the problem. You shouldn't be jealous of each other. It just don't make no sense. You should be glad somebody else is doing good. I tell 'em all the time I'm glad.*

I haven't talked to Dre since '91. I've talked to Cube since the funeral a couple times. I haven't seen him since '89. And Ren, he lives two blocks away from me and I ain't really seen him. You know, everybody has just been doing they own little thing. It's nothing bad, but it's just — you know, everybody doing four different careers.

Jerry Heller: *I see Dre all the time. Social, you know, "Hey, how you doing?" We're filling up our cars at the gas station or whatever. His mom lives two streets over, I'm very close friends with his mother. His sister had twins on Martin Luther King's birthday. Verna, I see her in the market, we say hello or whatever. I'm very friendly with his family.*

Yella: *You know, it's kind of crazy but I am a person I will not bug nobody. Or be all up in your face. So when I seen Dre last week I told him, I said, "I'm here for us. Not here because I'm trying to get you to do something or ask you for something. Nah, that ain't me." I said, "Man, I would never come ask you for a nickel. I will go broke before I go back begging for money for that." That just not me. Just like Cube. I tried to see him. See if me and him is supposed to hook up and see each other. I said, "Man, we should just talk. This ain't about business or nothing. It's just old times, but that never happened. So... you know.*

Me and him just met just to meet. I happen to get his number from somebody and we talked and we just met at a restaurant and we sat and talked three-four hours. Yeah, it was nobody around us, it was just me and him. Talking about all the old times and all kind of little things. He's definitely going through a lot of shit right now [Laughing]. But you know, he told me all about it... just everything. That's how me and him was. Me and him was friends way before Eazy was.

Jerry Heller: Basically, he's a very non-confrontational guy. When it comes to stuff like that, he's a very sensitive, non-confrontational kind of guy and he basically has turned into a recluse. I think that, I never --- I misjudged the fact that I never thought that anyone could come between Eazy and Dre, they were that close. I take that as a personal failure, and not protecting Eazy's assets, of course, and his biggest asset was Andre Young. So, you know, I sort of take that as a personal failure.

Yella: I live in a city called Corona. That's like in Riverside. It's like, probably 40-50 minutes outside of L.A. Just get away from all the crazy stuff in the city. A lot of people are moving out there now. Ren live like two blocks away, but I ain't seen him [Laughing]. And he live right around the corner.

CHAPTER 13

JERRY HELLER COMES TO FACE THE GAME

Jayceon Terrell Taylor, aka The Game, grew up in Compton, California. His father was a Nutty Block Crip and his mother a Hoover Crippelette. Life was tough; he was placed in foster care at the age of 7. He left the system at the age of 15 to live with his mother and was indoctrinated into the Bloods in a Crip neighbourhood by his brother, who carved out his own reputation on the streets as Big Fase 100 and led the Cedar Block Piru Bloods. He graduated from Compton High School in 1999 and was allegedly awarded a Basketball scholarship at Washington State University and expelled for drug possession, though the University denies he was ever enrolled. He then spent the next two years hustling on the streets until being shot five times in Los Angeles suburb Bellflower over a deal gone bad, resulting in a three-day coma.

Taylor began to rap and built a reputation on the mixtape scene in L.A. and The Bay as The Game, signing with indie label Get Low Records in 2002 on the strength of his You Know What It Is Vol. 1 mixtape. The tape captured the attention of Los Angeles son and all-star NBA point guard Baron Davis, he placed it with Diddy, who came close to signing him, and months later Dr. Dre who signed him in 2003. Dr. Dre then placed his new sensation 50 Cent with The Game making a brief appearance in the January 2003 classic "In Da Club" video and continued to mentor him. The Game stayed, building his reputation on the streets with key guest spots and mixtape releases, holding enough weight and buzz to be featured in an ad for Sean John and a Boost Mobile commercial alongside Kanye West and Ludacris.

The Game - You Know What It Is Vol. 1 (http://www.datpiff.com/The-Game-You-know-what-it-is-vol-1-mixtape.494.html)

His official arrival and introductory major label release came armed with the co-sign of both Dr. Dre and 50 Cent via G-Unit/Aftermath/Interscope in the form of the #93 Billboard Top 100 Single "Westside Story" on September 7, 2004. It was co-produced by Dr. Dre and Scott Storch, and was co-written by Mike Elizondo, Dre, Storch, The Game and 50 Cent. Get Low Records followed up with the release of The Game's mobbed out Untold Story album on October 5, 2004. Dr. Dre promptly put The Game back on pace with the release of the #4 Billboard Top 100 Single "How We Do" featuring 50 Cent on November 23, 2004. The Game album The Documentary came on January 28, 1995 and debuted at #1 on the Billboard Top 200 selling 586 000 copies its first week. It was immediately trailed by the "Hate It Or Love It" single, again featuring 50 Cent, on January 28, 2005, that peaked at #2 on the Billboard Top 100 Singles chart for five weeks. The Game had game and he was set.

In the exclusive 2006 interview with Jerry Heller, he addressed rappers who attacked him in diss songs and spoke on the time he came to face The Game.

Jerry Heller: *I'm happy that Eazy and I were able to provide a springboard or a forum or whatever for these people to become enormously successful and enormously rich. And it's funny when I think about it because in XXL they listed the 20 biggest diss records of all-time; two were about me and I'm a businessman. I always thought that was funny. But this year, besides those two records, Game had out a diss record about me and Nelly did ("Spida Man") I do take issue with that* because Dre and Cube, above everything else, they know me. I was their manager; I was their record company. Dre grew up with Jerry Heller being his father figure. I was; these guys know me so if they wanna say something bad about me, I'm not saying what they are saying is right, but they've earned that privilege. Sure, they're wrong about what they say, but at least they've earned the right, they do know me. Nelly, who is he that he can write about me? I don't know him. I've never met him. He hasn't earned that right, and one day I ran into Game.

It's hard for me to dislike Game, he has a picture of Eazy-E tattooed on his forearm. He has N.W.A across his chest, Compton across his neck and his face. It's hard for me to have any kind of animosity toward him but I was with my cousin and one of the old Ruthless bodyguards that's now an animator, and the head of Warner Brothers. We were down at the Galleria at a Starbucks, just sitting outside and I was trying to make an animation deal for Animal at Warner Brothers and Game walked by. I said to Animal "Who is that guy?" and he said, "I don't know." I said, "Tell him to come over here because he has something on his mind" because I always know. I hung out with Eazy enough to know when people go out of their way to ignore you that when he walked by, it was like the second time he walked by.

So he came over and we talked for a couple of hours and at the end I said, "You know, you really have a lot of fucking nerve. You're talking shit about me in your song. I mean, why would you write a song about me like that?" and he said "I thought it was a compliment. I thought you'd like it." So I just let it go at that because of; the guy loves Eazy-E, he loves N.W.A, he loves Compton. I think he's probably the most talented west coast rapper out there now so I give him his respect and his props. So I just let it go. I said, "Oh, okay". So we talk once in while. He'll call me, he called me from Europe a couple of weeks ago, or I'll call him or something and we'll just talk about something but I like him. I like Game.

CHAPTER 14
THE LEGACY

The rich legacy of N.W.A grows every year. Its tree grows stronger roots and bears new fruit each and every time a member of the group creates or introduces a new talent, project, or product for the world to behold. Every member has released solo recordings, contributed to new music with lyrics or production, and toured as an artist or DJ. The entrepreneurial spirit of Dr. Dre and Ice Cube has earned them well over a billion dollars. The critically acclaimed box office smash film Straight Outta Compton, documenting their early years, has enraptured a new generation of fans. Sadly, Eazy-E's children have lived most of their lives without a father, and the once mighty Ruthless Records is a mere shadow of its former colossal self.

Yella and Jerry Heller spoke on the legacy of N.W.A, Eazy-E's children and the state of Ruthless Records following the death of Eric "Eazy-E" Wright.

Yella: I just collected another check just a week ago. I'm still collecting money off of that. You would be amazed [Laughing]. It still sells. I mean, it's been selling for so long. I'm still getting checks from '89. You know, from stuff in '89. It just — that music was so different. And it just — the group was like The Beatles. So different, you know, it just hangs around. So right now I'm fittin' to do the N.W.A Greatest Hits, put that compilation together.

Jerry Heller: *I think that Eazy and I were responsible for guys like 50 Cent now and all those guys that have their own little entities and the fact that everybody has gotten enormously rich, which is the way it should be because as rich as people used to get, none of them had 50-storey buildings at the corner of 52nd & 6th Avenue. Because I have always felt and thought that the record companies were the robber barons of our generation, same as the railroad guys were in the 1800s.*

Yella: *His son Eric is my Godson. I take care of him already. But I'm setting up something for his kids because his kids ain't getting taken care of. I don't live with him but like Christmas time I bought him all his gifts, school clothes and stuff like that. I've been his Godfather ever since he was born like in '90 or '89. I think it was '89, so it wasn't like an overnight Godparent. I had already been there but I take care of him all the time.*

Jerry Heller: *I've talked to him (Lil' Eazy) twice in my life. I never knew him when he was young. I met him about, I guess, maybe a year and a half ago when he was recording for Virgin with Pete Farmer. I met him at Marie Callender's down on Wilshire and we talked for a few minutes. We didn't talk about anything substantial.*

Yella: *The courts and lawyers, they'll be going to court for years probably. Just trying to decide what to do with it, who owns it, and whatever they're going too. But the lawyers are getting paid so by the time they finish, you know... There's going to be nothing. It may be a little bit from these new records and the Bone new stuff and all of that, but they — I don't think they going to court — it ain't about his kids. That's for sure. It's just about the company.*

Jerry Heller: *I told him if he went and got some acting lessons that I probably could find a place for him in the Ruthless movie that I'm gonna do, and we had a reasonably pleasant conversation, and I met him once more in a studio and they've called me a couple of times and I've called them but basically, I didn't know him then. Eric never brought* him around, so I didn't really know him. I did know several of his children because I was sort of responsible for their private schools and their birthday parties, things like that because he was very attached to his children, but I had never met 'Lil E and really, I don't know what to say about him

Yella: It was quite a few things that weren't released that could — like, Eazy, I got a song from him that I haven't turned in. I still got it. That was one of his last songs. I think I'm just going to keep it. A trophy or something. I was supposed to have been able to use it but at the last second I can't use it. I got a Bone song. They just... I don't know what they problem is. I don't even deal with them so; I mean, you know, Ruthless' name is there but Ruthless is gone. The real Ruthless is buried somewhere in Whittier. It's all about business now. I gotta go — when I write, I don't deal with them but like on the Eazy album I had to deal with them, business.

Jerry Heller: I can't talk about that (the state of Ruthless Records). But you know what it was then and you know what it is now, so you gotta make your own determinations. But it does make me real sad.

Yella: You know, it's just a shame. When somebody dies vultures come out. I mean, I don't care if it's just the average person on the street. If you got a little something, somebody wants it, yeah, always. It's amazing.

July 4, 2000 UP IN SMOKE TOUR AFTER-PARTY Toronto, Canada

CHAPTER 15
BRUCE WILLIS

A film documenting the life and times of N.W.A was rumoured for many years. In 2015, it became a reality with the F. Gary Gray directed major motion picture Straight Outta Compton finally coming to life on the big screen. To date, the film has grossed over $200 000 000 worldwide. It has also served as the catalyst for Dr. Dre to deliver his first solo album since the 1999 release of 2001 with the companion piece of music inspired by the film, Compton.

Produced by Ice Cube, Tomica Woods-Wright, Matt Alvarez, F. Gary Gray, Scott Bernstein, and Dr. Dre, in tune with the legacy of N.W.A, its release did not come without controversy. Ice Cube's son, O'Shea Jackson Jr., was awarded the opportunity to play his father in the film and while Lil Eazy-E was rumoured to be a lock to play his father, his acting chops failed to meet the criteria and it was not to be. A casting call for female extras became embroiled with charges of sexism, racism, and colourism of Black women. On August 14, 2014, a drive-by shooting occurred perilously close to the set in front of the Compton courthouse, complete with flashing gang signs and a stray bullet striking an on-looking pedestrian. Then on January 29, 2015, Suge Knight infamously arrived on set and in a cornered fit of rage ran over and killed his friend, Terry Carter, and mangled the foot of filmmaker Cle Sloan, who also suffered head injuries.

The film ran 147 minutes, and there was still a lot of key people, who were intrinsically involved with the rise of N.W.A that were either ignored or misrepresented in the retelling of the tale and expressed their displeasure. In reality, founding member, Arabian Prince, who is pictured on the Straight Outta Compton album cover, was present for half the scenes in the film when they occurred in real life, yet swept under the carpet with an uncredited cameo. The MC Ren character was presented as a side-note and rarely spoke in the film. World Class Wrecking Cru impresario Alonzo Williams noted several factual inaccuracies, citing gangster music did not exist when the scenes depicting him directing Dre and Yella to not play the music actually happened. He also states that he was the one to introduce Eazy-E and Jerry Heller, a fact confirmed in the 2006 Heller book Ruthless: A Memoir.

Arabian Prince Reveals Discrepancies In Straight Outta Compton (https://youtu.be/s1mIDSgEoVg)

Alonzo Williams Talks Wreckin Cru, Eazy-E, Ice Cube, N.W.A and Straight Outta Compton Movie (https://youtu.be/azr0Ah5J6gU)

MC Ren comments on the accuracy of Straight Outta Compton (https://youtu.be/B3p7BV53m-g)

Obviously not proud of his own violent past episodes of misogyny and definitely not a good look for the most successful man to ever pick up a mic and rap, Dr. Dre saw to it that his early abusive relationships and the children they beget were not mentioned in the film. Notably his tumultuous violent relationship with singer Michel'le, with whom he shares a son, Marcel, and parted together from Ruthless Records to Death Row Records that ended up married to Suge Knight. Nor was there any mention of the infamous January 27, 1991 episode of Dr. Dre beating up Dee Barnes inside a restaurant washroom following her late 1990 interview with Ice Cube on Fox's weekly TV series Pump It Up that painted an unsavoury portrayal of N.W.A. Though Dr. Dre did issue a public statement on August 21, 2015 expressing regret and apologizing to the women he had hurt, coincidentally the day before Apple announced it had purchased one of his investments, Beats Electronics, for $3 billion and made him an executive.

'The Vlad Couch' Ft. Michel'le
(https://youtu.be/ky0A3bGPqnE)

Ice Cube on Pump It Up with Dee Barnes
(https://youtu.be/FcQgZ3IyVHg)

Dee Barnes On The Assault That Was Left Out Of 'Straight Outta Compton
(https://youtu.be/mcaqWIMtso4)

Then, on October 30, 2015, Jerry Heller resurfaced and filed a 12-claim lawsuit against NBCUniversal, director F. Gary Gray, Legendary Pictures, the screenwriters of the film, Ice Cube, Dr. Dre and the estate of Eazy-E.

Yella had alluded to an N.W.A film in his exclusive 1996 interview. Jerry Heller also spoke on an N.W.A film in his 2006 exclusive interview, stating that he had already found the money to produce it and casting and filming was set to begin sometime in 2007. He then went on to name and list several people he would like to see up for the roles of N.W.A and himself in the big screen version of his story, Ruthless.

Yella: I think we're gonna write a movie, N.W.A movie.

Jerry Heller: I'm gonna do a movie. Just those ten years of Ruthless. It's the Ruthless story and I have a script and I've talked to a number of people, and interviewing Directors now. The money is up so; it's a 20 million dollar movie and we're gonna start filming, probably around the beginning of January.

Yella: I think we going to split it five ways, so Eazy's share gonna go to his kids to try and help them. So, Dre brought that up to me the other day when I talked to him.

Jerry Heller: I have no contact with any of them so I don't know what they think and I could really care less what any of them; it doesn't matter to me. I'm gonna do what I'm gonna do for Ruthless and for him, and just like Jerry Heller, they were just players in the whole scheme of things.

So I would like Larenz Tate to play Eazy. I think he's a wonderful actor and I look in his eyes and I see Eazy there, and I would like to see; I would like Terence Howard to play Dr. Dre, and I've talked to Game several times about playing Suge Knight and I saw him in Waist Deep or Waist High, or whatever it was and I thought even though he had a small part, I thought he was a very powerful presence on the screen, and I think that if he bulked up a little he could play Suge Knight. And Jessica Simpson could play my wife, and I've talked to Bruce Willis about playing my part although I've talked to other people also.

You know when you do movies, it's different. It's not the same as doing a record because now you're talking about what box office value is of people overseas because you're looking for sixty percent of the financing comes from overseas and you gotta have people that have box office cache in the rest of the world, and Bruce Willis is a guy, you know, who I think could play the part well although, you know, I'm gonna have to teach him how to be a little more Jewish. But I think that he could play the part well and he has a lot of cache throughout the world. He's a big, big name, and I've talked to other people. And then in the movie business it's about when people are available and when they're not available, and you know, who this investor likes and who this investor likes.

You're doing a one-time movie and you know, you have to just have to do it for the moment. You have to seize the moment. Carpe Diem or whatever, that's what you have to do. I'm sort of flexible about it. I thought that Allen Iverson would be a great Eazy-E but he's, you know, he's 6"2 and got a job, so it's not that easy but he's the kind of rebel that Eazy was and I like him. Who knows if he can act or not. So those are sort of the people that I'm thinking about.

Jerry Heller: The most important part is done; we have the money *so – In the film business, you got the money then it's just a matter of who is available and who isn't and whether they get along and stuff like that, so it's gonna happen. I'm not sure about the – I'm not sure about the chronological order, it's my first movie I've ever been involved with.*

Issue #48 Winter 1999

CHAPTER 16
CHRONIC 2001

D r. Dre finally resurfaced with the long-awaited follow-up to his seminal album, The Chronic, on November 16, 1999 with 2001. Initially slated to be released as Chronic 2000, Suge Knight, who still had it out for his former partner, enlisted his roster of artists to produce new songs and pulled from the extensive Death Row Records unreleased back catalogue to release the double-disc set, Suge Knight Represents: Chronic 2000, on April 27, 1999.

Dr. Dre simply dusted the dirt off his shoulder and set to work, fine-tuning his return to action. A classic album in its own right, 2001 flowed like fine wine replete with a refined version of the beloved G-Funk he first delivered to the masses seven years prior on The Chronic.

Snoop Dogg was back in the fold and as dangerous as ever, his compatriots Nate Dogg and Kurupt along for the ride. MC Ren dropped knowledge. New sensation, Eminem, scorched the earth on his songs. An assortment of known and upcoming artists were invited to touch the mic and contribute too. Actor Eddie Griffin and porn star, Jake Steed, had interludes. Mary J. Blige closed out the album in classy fashion over lush Lord Finesse production.

In this exclusive 1999 interview with Dr. Dre that occurred in a mid-town Manhattan Hotel room, he spoke on his state of mind, karma, and spirituality, and let us in on why he said, "Fuck rap!"

What's on your mind?

Dr. Dre: *What's on my mind? What do you mean, right now? Basically just chillin' out. This is actually a real laid back day for me. I just get to sit here in the hotel and talk about me (laughter).*

Is there a Dr. Dre state of mind?

Dr. Dre: *Actually there is. It's funny you ask me that because I never really thought about it, at the same time there is. Dr. Dre, I mean, I want to handle my business; I'm a fiend for handling my business and making music, that's it. I'm three things: I have to be in a state of mind where my family is straight and everything around me has got to be straight. I can't even sleep if the room is messy. That's my state of mind, straight up. Everything around me has to be perfect.*

Therefore, fine tuning the styles and making songs until you're happy and then putting the album together.

Dr. Dre: *Straight up. No doubt about it.*

Do you have something to prove with this album?

Dr. Dre: *I think so. That was my motivation actually going in the studio because over the last couple of years there was a lot of people saying that Dre doesn't have it anymore, or he fell off and what have you. This record is for them. This is my shut the fuck up album! Straight up.*

Is revenge one of the states of mentality on this album?

Dr. Dre: *I wouldn't say it's revenge. It's basically like I said, it's the shut the fuck up album. I had a couple of years where --- Actually it was like this: I got married and my music softened up a little bit because I felt funny saying the lyrics that I was saying and being married and being a family man, but my wife actually was the motivation for me to* *get back to doing what I do, hardcore dirty Hip-Hop, straight up. I'm just happy doing that.*

Did you make any sacrifices?

Dr. Dre: *None at all. No sacrifices were made for this. The only thing I had to do, man, was go in there and do my thing and I had the support of a lot of good people.*

In the past was there a conspiracy out to get you, were people ganging up against you?

Dr. Dre: *No, I don't think that. I believe I was my own worst enemy. You talking about just musically or just in general? In general, I mean; no. I just had to go in and do my thing. First of all, I have to feel like I'm having fun with it, having fun period. Every day of my life I have to be having fun and I have to feel good, so that's it.*

The music has always been there. Why do people say you fell off?

Dr. Dre: *You know what it is? My separation with Death Row. I ain't even answered your last questions correctly, I'll get to that but my last record --- My separation with Death Row I put a record out called Dr. Dre Presents The Aftermath, which was a good record in my opinion, it just wasn't what people wanted at that time. The record went platinum, but people wanted this record that I'm putting out now. I think that's where all the criticism came from.*

There was darkness. Every move somebody made was to put you down. Spreading rumours that you're gay. Suge Knight marrying Michele'le. Daz talking all this shit about you. What was going through your mind when this was happening?

Dr. Dre: *Nothing. That is absolute nonsense that doesn't make my heart pump any faster. It has no relevance to me. I heard it but it's just in one ear and out the other, straight up.*

Is this why Daz is not on the album and Kurupt is?

Dr. Dre: *Correct. Definitely. Either you ride with me or you're not. It's as simple as that. He chose to do his thing that way and Kurupt is a real good friend of mine.*

What's you take on "Callin' Out Names" and all the violence? A bodyguard getting killed, Kurupt attacked and all that nonsense?

Dr. Dre: *I don't condone that at all. I'm not really into that, man, the disrespect game or nothing like that. I'm done with that. People are getting seriously hurt behind that, and like I said, I don't condone it. It's just crazy. He has his personal beefs with certain people and what have you and he's gonna talk about it. That's his thing. I have absolutely nothing to do with that.*

There is a part on the album where you say "Fuck Rap". Break it down.

Dr. Dre: *I basically say that because of all the criticism I got while I was making this record, and I say it because I feel like this is gonna be like my last solo album. I'm thirty-four years old now. I can't see myself waiting another seven years being forty-years old and making a Hip-Hop album. I'm never gonna stop producing. I'll be producing records for as long as I can turn knobs. As far as me being in the limelight this will be it for me.*

Dr. Dre featuring Eminem - "Forgot About Dre" (https://youtu.be/OVYDtOtpVVw)

Why? When you know you can keep doing it and you know you don't have to wait seven years.

Dr. Dre: *Well, for me to get motivated it probably would take that long for me to just say, 'Okay, I'm gonna do another Dr. Dre album.' I don't need to. I can go and scout out artists. That's what I really like doing. I like producing. I don't really like being an artist. I like being behind the scenes producing, directing videos and what have you. I can do that forever and I don't have to have a certain look or a certain way of carrying myself to the public to do that.*

But you always put across the same dark and deep imagery.

Dr. Dre: *Definitely. Still I don't see myself being out there like that and another whatever. I don't see it happening. It would have to be something real dramatic that happens to make me go in the studio and do another Dr. Dre album.*

Do you believe in karma?

Dr. Dre: *Definitely. Definitely believe in karma, straight up.*

Do you want to expound on that?

Dr. Dre: *I just believe in it this way; what goes around comes around. I definitely believe that, seriously. I've seen cases that people do dirt to people and some way, it might not be the same thing that happens, it might not be the same thing that they did to that person but something goes wrong. It never fails, at least in my eyes. I guess that answers your question.*

Are you a spiritual person?

Dr. Dre: *Yes, yes. I actually grew up as a; when I was younger I grew up in the Church, Baptist Church. I used to go to Church all the time with my Grandmother. I definitely believe in God and I definitely believe in Heaven and Hell. That's just my vibe.*

Where are you going?

Dr. Dre: *Hopefully Heaven. I believe I've lived a pretty cool life. I've never done anything intentionally wrong to somebody, or... I really believe I have a chance to pass through those gates, seriously.*

And what will happen to those who have done you wrong?

Dr. Dre: *I don't know. It depends on how they're living their lives, straight up. Just because --- I'm not God. Just because somebody has done or said something wrong to me doesn't make them a person that's not righteous. They could have been having a bad day, who knows?*

How old are your children?

Dr. Dre: *I really don't like to talk about my children, or get intimate like that. We'll keep it on the business.*

What is it like when Dre hangs out in L.A.? Can you walk the streets of L.A.?

Dr. Dre: *Definitely, definitely can walk the streets of L.A. I mean, there's certain parts of L.A. that I won't walk 'cause there are people out there that I feel like as hard as you work for your money there's ten other people out there working just as hard to get it from you. You have to watch your back and that's with anywhere though. I love L.A. I wouldn't live any other place.*

What about C.J. Mac, Rollin' 60's, talking shit about you on his album, King of L.A., and all that?

Dr. Dre: *You know, I heard about it, I haven't heard it so I really can't comment on it as well as I would like to. That's nonsense. I heard he said something about me saying gangster rap is dead and then getting back into it or whatever, something to that nature. My take on that is basically this: how is anyone gonna speak on something that I invented, period.*

Who has picked up the torch?

Dr. Dre: *What torch?*

Who is carrying on the tradition of Gangster Rap? Who do you see as your peers?

Dr. Dre: *I don't even like that term to tell you the truth, Gangster Rap. To be perfectly honest with you, there's absolutely nothing out there that I'm really, really feeling like that. That's the kind of music that we started. There's nothing, so I would have to say nobody's picked up the torch.*

No one in the South has a sound that's for you?

Dr. Dre: *There are records that I like. There are records that I like but there is no like big Hip-Hop superstar out there right now. The way me and Snoop hit it. The way Biggie Smalls did it. The way Tupac did it. There is no big superstar out there right now. Again, I'm gonna say nobody has picked that torch up.*

Why?

Dr. Dre: *I don't know. Hopefully November 16th I'll be picking it back up. It's just that --- I don't know, I don't know. Maybe it's the music, maybe it's the personalities, maybe it's ... I don't know. I have no idea.*

Is it because no one truly knows the pulse of America? Do you know the pulse of America? Or is what you're feeling the pulse of America?

Dr. Dre: *Well, I actually don't even think about it that deep. I really go in the studio and just make the kind of record that I feel like making that day. It's whatever comes out that day. I rarely think about what I'm gonna do until I get in the studio.*

Were you mad at your wife when "Hoe's A Housewife" was written?

Dr. Dre: *Nah, I actually didn't write that song, Kurupt did. I'm never mad at my wife, at all. That was actually a song that he was talking about some guy that he knows, something like that, that was moving this girl into his house or something like that, that was a known slut, so that's what motivated that song.*

Who is your clique these days? Who do you hang with?

Dr. Dre: *I basically probably can count the people that I hang out with on one hand. I basically hang out with just the people that I work with, period. When I'm not with them I'm with my family. It's basically just a couple of guys that I have who are talent scouting for me and work and stuff like that. A guy that co-produced the album with me named Mel-Man, and also just the artists that I work with. I don't have friends that just hang out. I don't do it like that.*

What went wrong with Aftermath after the compilation was dropped? All these album that were supposed to drop and the King Tee never coming out. Then all of a sudden a quick fix with Eminem and boom! You're back on the map larger than ever.

Dr. Dre: *What went wrong was basically me. I got comfortable. I got married. I wasn't in the studio as much as I should have been. The tracks that I was doing were sounding a little different. So, I wasn't happy about it, so I wasn't putting out any product. On the compilation, Dr. Dre Presents The Aftermath, I only produced and performed on one song. The King Tee record, I did a couple of songs on his record that I wasn't happy about and the rest of the stuff on his album I don't think he was real happy about, so that got pushed. I'm definitely gonna get back in there and make something happen now that I'm back on point. It was just a period of my life that I had to just take a little break, that's all.*

What was the decision behind piercing your tongue?

Dr. Dre: *This was done, actually, me and my wife did it on our third anniversary. This was something we decided to do. We got back in town from our anniversary trip in Hawaii and went right to the body piercing shop. "This is what we gonna do. This is gonna represent our third anniversary".*

What else do you want to get out there? Is there anything else you want to say?

Dr. Dre: *It sounds like it went pretty well. This was a different one. I like that.*

Just wakin up in the mornin gotta thank God
I don't know but today seems kinda odd
No barkin from the dog, no smog
And momma cooked a breakfast with no hog
(damn)
I got my grub on, but didn't pig out
Finally got a call from a girl I wanna dig out
(Whassup?) Hooked it up for later as I hit the do'
Thinkin will I live, another twenty-fo'
I gotta go cause I got me a drop top
And if I hit the switch, I can make the ass drop
Had to stop, at a red light
Lookin in my mirror and not a jacker in sight
And everything is alright
I got a beep from Kim, and she can fuck all night
Called up the homies and I'm askin y'all
Which park, are y'all playin basketball?
Get me on the court and I'm trouble
Last week fucked around and got a triple double
Freakin niggaz everyway like M.J.
I can't believe, today was a good day (shit!)

Ice Cube – *"It Was A Good Day"*

photo by Harris Rosen
Westside Connection TERRORIST THREATS Fall 2003 New York, New York

CHAPTER 17
ICE CUBE: I'LL REST WHEN I'M DEAD

n 2001 Ice Cube was fourteen films into his celluloid career and on the verge of crossing over to mainstream acceptance with the upcoming release of the first film in the BarberShop series. In this exclusive interview from inside his trailer on the set of the final installment of the Friday series, Friday After Next, he reflected on his music career prior to the scheduled release of his Greatest Hits album on December 4, 2001.

Juggling raps since he was fourteen and filling the big screen for over a decade, you'd think that Ice Cube would have pushed his boundaries by now. Solo or in a crew, he's dropped more platinum-selling albums than most of his microphone peers could dream of, taken popular music hostage on a number of recorded sieges, and conditionally re-negotiated the way middle America understands ghetto living in 1988 with N.W.A's Straight Outta Compton and his 1990 solo debut, Amerikkka's Most Wanted. On the hit list of common decency from the day those records hit stores, sold millions, and ended up in the hands of impressionable youth, Cube was immediately cast as gangster rap's preeminent criminal icon.

From one territory to another, he managed to parlay that success and status into Hollywood currency and a resume that rivals his career in music: he's directed over twenty music videos; he's starred in feature films, including his seminal debut, Boyz N the Hood; and he's acted in, written, and directed his own Cube Vision productions of Friday, Next Friday, and The Players' Club. In production with co-star Mike Epps on the set of the third installment of the Friday series, Friday After Next (released on November 22, 2002), Cube is sitting back from the rap game, releasing his Greatest Hits collection, considering the next collaboration steps, and shopping for a label that can handle his business.

You have had an extremely long and successful career, and obviously you've changed, grown, and have different mindsets. What do you have to say to those who think they know what you have become?

Ice Cube: This happens with everybody. I think my work speaks for itself. My work said whatever I feel about what I'm doin'. You can't really think about detractors. Everybody's gonna have critics. Once you out here as long as I've been you not gonna be able to please everybody in Hip-Hop. You're not gonna be able to please everybody in the movie business. It's just really all about staying consistent, doing what I like, doing what I'm into. People always want me to do the records that I used to do, but that to me is a waste of time. It's kind of like if you want to hear what I think on certain topics go get Death Certificate, go get Amerikkka's Most Wanted, go get The Predator, go get Lethal Injection. Them records, I don't see no need to do 'em over. The kids out now is just a regurgitated version of what we used to do, just flipped. I always look for either you're an Ice Cube fan or you're not, and I'm not trying to get people who know I'm just down with what I'm doing.

What's the present status of Heavyweight?

Ice Cube: I wouldn't know. I stopped fuckin' with Heavyweight in 1997. The first album released that I was involved with was the Player's Club and that was the last. I broke away from Heavyweight because I didn't like the people that was involved in it. I haven't been involved in what's going on in that company for three or four years now.

You did Da Lench Mob as well as Kausion and K-Dee. You started as an artist and went into music naturally. How did your film and Directing career take more of a presence?

Ice Cube: The Rap game to me is like you start off in the Rap game, you in it for a little while, you kind of get played out. It's like the same 'ole shit, same 'ole interviews, same 'ol go to radio stations, same 'ole shit begging people to buy your record, same old record company shit. It's kind of like being in a league, being in the NBA or NFL. I've been in this shit since I was fifteen years old. I've been trying to push raps. I'm thirty-two now, so that's seventeen years of rhymin', fourteen actually. I mean fourteen years old is when I started. You got all this time that I've been in the game and your creative juices only flow so long in that area. If you're a true artist you're gonna want to expand your vision. I think the pleasure I used to get out of writing five-minute rhymes and records, I get that same pleasure writing a two hour movie. Its been more creative on a bigger scale visually, audio, everything. It's being able to show what you got not just on the radio, but visual.

You outlasted Priority Records. No one would have thought that.

Ice Cube: Hmmm, I would have. They was just rolling on our juice from day one. I'm a free agent now after this Greatest Hits album. I can go sign with whoever I want too. That label wasn't able to sell records and wasn't able to make things as big as they should be. Sometimes it's not the records you do but the label you on. When you going against Interscope or Def Jam putting millions of dollars in their campaign compared to Priority trying to do this shit for three of four hundred thousand, you can't compete in the marketplace after a while. That's what I've been dealing with all these years is I've been on an inferior label who couldn't sell what I was pushin'.

Weight?

Ice Cube: Well, you know, whatever. I always dig the records I do.

Everybody's not gonna dig every record that you do. I expect that, but I always had a few on the album that real Hip-Hop heads can get with, so I'm satisfied with that. See, I'm not trying to get the whole pie. I just want my piece. I'm not trying to sell ten million records for some fuckin' record company. They get the lion's share of that shit.

Everybody wants their success when their name is out there and everybody wants a piece of them because their name brings in dollars. A lot of people get those lines extended but you are one of a handful who delivers and has been able to capitalize, for better or worse.

Ice Cube: *One thing, whether you like the projects or dislike the projects, I always thought there was a sense of quality in there that anybody could appreciate. You not gonna like every piece of art a person do. That shit not realistic, but you go and see the time and effort I put into the shit, that I wasn't just throwin' anything out there like I don't care about it. I like what I do. I've made a lot of money, so it's not like I'm in it to get paid. It ain't like I'm in it to get paid. I am paid! It's kind of like I'm in it to do what I like to do, and I've been in it doin' shit to get paid, to keep it crackin'. Now I'm at a point in my life where I can just do it as I feel it and do what I like. Sometimes I'm gonna make mistakes but that's any artist. Any artist that's true is gonna try to push the envelope. See how good he really is. See what he really can do and what he really can't do.*

What was going through your mind while compiling the Greatest Hits?

Ice Cube: *Getting one or two good songs off of each album. That was the main focus 'cause I have so many I knew that I'm gonna miss some people's greatest hits. But I can always come out with a volume two. I've got a lot of stuff. That to me was like the first issue; if you really want to know what Cube is about from day one until now then you have it.*

Do you care about the present state of Hip-Hop, or is it just Ice Cube doin' his own thing?

Ice Cube: Ice Cube doin' his own thing. I'm too old to be worried about that shit. I'm too old to be worried about who battlin' who and who got the best rhyme and what crews goin' against that crew. That shit is for kids, man. I respect Hip-Hop to the fullest. I won't sit here and let you think I'm shitting on it as I respect it to the fullest. But it's kind of like it's its own fuckin' animal. You really got to get dirty to benefit all the way off the game. I've paid my dues. I just do shit for Ice Cube fans, not for Hip-Hop fans.

Do you ever think back to the days of N.W.A and how your career progressed? All the things you said and did that were significant; you were the real public enemy.

Ice Cube: Yeah. I mean, anybody would take time to reflect because it's me. I mean, it's me but it's still awesome to see and to live and to think back on. But I don't spend a whole lot of time dwelling on that because I think I got so much to do. I don't think I've reached my ceiling yet as far as what I'm gonna do, what I'm gonna mean to a lot of the generations. It's just a lot of work to be done. I'll rest when I'm dead.

Any regrets with your music career?

Ice Cube: Oh yeah, there's a few. Anybody that can say that they've been in the game without any regrets is lying. I'm not gonna point 'em out because I think it's just for me to know not to do this or do that again. Everybody has regrets.

What are you most proud of?

Ice Cube: My longevity in this game. This is a quick game to be in and out. To be able to release a Greatest Hits and still be able to do a new album without people saying. No matter what, people are gonna check for what Cube got to say. Whether it's your favourite record or not, they're still gonna check it 'cause I'm always saying something other than just the norm.

Westside Connection, Heltah Skeltah, N.W.A Will any of these projects happen?

Ice Cube: The only thing I can really be positive on is Westside Connection. You know that's gonna happen. That's the next record I want to do. But like I said, I'm changing labels right now. So until I land somewhere we're not gonna start that project because everybody has to be in total agreement before we get going. Business is really hampering our start, which is cool because I don't have time right now to do it. But it's comin'. I don't know about the N.W.A stuff. That's on Dre. He's had some mega-hits these last two years with his record and then the Eminem record, so I don't know. Whenever he's ready 'cause you can't do an N.W.A record without Dre producing the music. Until he call and say "Look, let's go in!"; we just waitin'.

Any message for Canada?

Ice Cube: Love Canada. Hate the border. Can't get my bud through. Tell them to ease up at that border and I'll be there a little more often.

Ice Cube is down with the P.E
Now every single bitch wanna see me
Big Daddy is smooth, word to mother
Let's check out a flick that exploits the color
Roaming through Hollywood late at night
Red and blue lights what a common sight
Pulled to the curb, getting played like a sucker
Don't fight the power...(gunshot)..the mother
fucker

Ice Cube – *"Burn Hollywood Burn"*

Photo by Harris Rosen
Mike Epps and Mary J. Blige at MARY party Toronto,
Canada 1999

CHAPTER 18

ICE CUBE: FROM BURNING TO TURNING HOLLYWOOD

A 2001 exclusive from the set of Friday After Next in Glendale, California, features separate behind the scenes interviews with Ice Cube and Mike Epps.

Picture a lone figure on stage gripping a mic in front of a packed and potentially hostile crowd. Just one in a string of guests for the night, he's spent the last half hour backstage, completely oblivious to who's been up before him and with little or no intel on the audience. They could be ready to open up and let it off or they could be your classic arms-crossed, screwface, show me your skills local mob. Maybe the last cat up on stage reached with words far iller than our guy's thesaurus can spit. Maybe, after dropping his dime on ladies jumping outta their seats and men who couldn't believe what they just heard, he just bounced off stage to thundering applause. In the back of his mind and at the front of any future pay cheque our guy knows it's a clash and, without any incriminating ballerina photos of the last man, it all comes down to skills - new material has to be tight, old material needs a fresh twist, and if he can't read and connect with the people it all could fall just shy of a bottling.

If you'll pardon the decks, turn up the lights, and put out the spliffs, there isn't much to separate the comedy and rap games. Mike Epps knows this. Having spent the better part of the mid-1990s working the Def Comedy Jam circuit and starring in two of HBO's Def Comedy Jam specials, he was 'discovered' at L.A.'s Comedy Store by Ice Cube who was, at the time, searching for a new comedy partner after Chris Tucker's career launched him beyond the scope of Cube's first film installment of the Friday series. Cast as cousin Day Day in Next Friday and, earlier this year, as Baby Powder in Method Man and Redman's How High, Epps' physical, spastic, and hyper-active routines easily match Tucker's manic energy. For Ice Cube, it's an essential ingredient to a proven formula. Like Big Boi and Dre, Flavor Flav and Chuck D, or even Erick and Parrish, sometimes the best comedy, like Hip Hop, comes in teams. Ice Cube knows this from working alongside the N.W.A cats and the Westside Connection crew. You know this from watching years of Abbott & Costello, Richard Pryor & Gene Wilder, or Walter Matthau & Jack Lemmon. And although he can write a joke, straight-man Ice Cube knows he can't personally deliver the comedy hits without Epps' gags.

"I think the dude is genuinely funny without trying to be," says Cube of his co-star. "You don't need to have a joke for him. He's just saying what he say and he's one of them dudes that's just fun to have around. The way he is on camera most of the time he's crazier in person. I just think he got it. Like Richard Pryor have it or Eddie Murphy have it. I saw that in Chris Tucker too and I had planned on creating some type of duo with that. But to be honest I'm glad it's with Mike because I think Mike needed it more than Chris. I like Mike better as a friend. Me and Chris, it was pretty much business."

Far more than a sidekick, Epps is part of an ensemble cast collected by Ice Cube that includes Clifton Powell, Don Curry, and John Witherspoon. In pooling the talent of all these comics, Cube has taken lessons learned from the market savvy studios of American Hip-

Hop to the big screen. Less ferocious than N.W.A, not quite as libidinous as Tha Dogg Pound, and just as dirty as the south, Cube's cast for his Friday series are like the Poon Tang Clan of Black American comedy. They're raunchy enough to get the big belly laughs, poignant enough to take more than a few political notes on life in South Central, and tight enough to bang out three installments with Friday, Next Friday, and the November release of Friday After Next. And while he can't boast rounds survived on the punishing U.S. comedy circuit, Ice Cube and his Cube Vision production company seem to have made the successful leap from dozens of music videos to full-length comedy features by applying a branded and controlling production philosophy he learned in the Rap game.

"I'm more of the orchestrator of all this," he says. "I can't play the flute and the horn but I can damn sure tell ya how to play it together to make a dope song. With Cube Vision I do push a creative control on it because I believe when you're trying to create a brand you gotta put your stamp on it or it's fraudulent. I want people to know that when they see Cube Vision they know the movie's gonna be good, period."

But taking the boasting points of a fifteen year rap career to the film world isn't necessarily gonna be a lock down and Cube's had his share of hot and not-so-hot screen shots. Under the wing of other production companies and other Directors, Cube's casting as the strong, silent type in Trespass, Anaconda, Three Kings, Higher Learning, and The Glass Shield all showcased the same raw talent John Singleton must have seen when he cast the rapper as Doughboy in Boyz 'N The Hood back in 1991. And with the circumspect, alpha-male type in high Hollywood demand these days, Cube can be picky about what roles he chooses and, more importantly, who he works with.

"I like to play characters that are solid," he says. "Characters that have strength to them. I want to play characters that I can be proud of. I don't want to look at no movies that I'm ashamed of. Then it's who the director is and what the story's about. That's definitely a big deal. [And] how much money is getting made. If you get all these things right you're lessening your chance to be in a wack movie. You play all your cards right you're lessening your chance to be in a fuckin' Ghosts of Mars or some shit. Sometimes you get it wrong. What can you do except to say that I have to get it right the next time."

For Cube, getting it right the next time generally means running the show yourself. With lessons learned working on John Carpenter's Martian flop, he's keeping future projects close to home and keeping his hands on everything from production to acting to writing to flipping the script with a first time Director on each of the Friday installments.

"As a Producer this is something like my baby," he says. "I don't want to work with a Director that's kinda set in his own ways. I don't want to be producing them and sitting in the background. I'm able to suggest things and he's more willing to do it than somebody who's done four or five movies and is like 'Well, yeah, but I wanna do it this way.' It's easy to work with because they got their own little edge. But they also willing to learn from me. These movies come with a certain kinda tone and a certain type of flavour and you gotta know that."

According to Epps, part of that flavour is Ice Cube's knack for tapping into the familiar - L.A. stories already ingrained into global popular culture through a decade of rap tales and a twist on a well-established American film genre.

"He has a style of comedy that is very familiar to Black people and white people and he don't have a problem expressing it," says Epps. "That Black cult movie. They're like Blaxploitation movies that will never be forgotten like Uptown Saturday Night and Piece of the Action."

The Friday's definitely have their share of freaks and playas. Clifton Powell plays Pinky, the retro pimped-out record store owner that shuttles around town in a pink stretch limo. The last time we saw Don Curry as Uncle Elroy he was tapped out on his supply of Viagra, relying instead on an impressive collection of dildos and Super 8 porn to get his girl going. And Katt Williams who goes by Money Mike, the newest member of the story in Friday After Next, runs a store called Pimps and Hoes in the mall where Craig and Day Day work security. But if Cube's hoping to transfer his multi-platinum success from the Rap game to the Hollywood game he's going to have to take lessons learned from Richard Pryor and Eddie Murphy. Only by opening up the Friday world beyond the confines of the hood will he truly break the bigger market. And that, according to co-star Don Curry, is all about finding your place through the script.

"With Ice Cube being a rapper people are surprised that he can write," he says. "But most of the effective rappers that I've known talk about reality; what they observe and what they feel. I think that shows up particularly in this script. It's reality pushed to the edge which makes it that much more fascinating or entertaining."

Whether or not Cube has applied such wisdom to the script of Friday After Next remains to be seen. Considering that over the last few years he's been more inclined towards turning rather than burning Hollywood, he's certainly capable of bringing a bigger, more complex world to the story. Later this month, in the action-comedy flick All About The Benjamins, we'll see how much America's once-most wanted can push his own envelope. Honing their one-on-one skills, Epps and Cube team up again as thief Reggie White and bounty hunter Bookem Jackson as the duo get tangled up in a Miami diamond heist. Cube says that the more they work together the funnier they get and that All About The Benjamins is "hella funny". Epps is a little more unpredictable and off-the-wall in his plug.

"You gone wanna sneak a steak sandwich when it comes out," he says. "You ain't gonna wanna get no popcorn. You gone wanna sneak in some double cheese burgers with some fries."

Like his Friday character, Epps is hard to get a serious fix on. If you ask him about the roles he's searching for he'll deadpan tell you his two years at DeVry have prepared him well.

"Nah, I'm just kidding," he says. "I'm trying to get some serious roles, try to break out of the little comedy mould for a minute. Hopefully I can do some of that Will Smith shit. They say I look a little like him. What do you think? From the side? If I look anything like Will Smith maybe they might give me something like his money."

Ask him about the moment when he realized he wanted to act more than work stand up. His answer?

"The other night when I realized that me and my baby's mama argue so much. I'm serious! Nah, I been realizing, man. I'm always up for a challenge and that's what I was looking for. I really want to challenge on the acting tip. It's time for me to get an opportunity for my talent and pool some other talent in 'cause I got an eye for it. I wanna show some of my expertise. And not to get too big for my britches but I think I got something bigger and better to offer than just what I'm bringing now. I'm in a rush to show that."

Or check into how he says fame has changed his fortune with the ladies since stepping off the comedy circuit into feature films.

"Believe it or not, I was a live wire before I got into the game," he says. "I always been live. I ain't gonna lie about that. Smell my fingers now if you don't believe me!"

Obviously, Cube's got lots to work with in Epps and wants to keep him close by, regardless of how much talent Epps thinks is locked away inside his head or how stinky his digits might be. Together, they bring a certain extended and constantly developing continuity that, if you rely on the greatest hits five-minutes on-stage approach of B.E.T.'s Comic View, is currently missing from Black American comedy. For his part, Epps says he's sticking with Cube Vision for project after project and that it's a fear of not being funny that constantly puts him over.

"It means, I'm gonna be Johnny on the spot," he says. "The day I lay off will be the day that I pay off. So I can't lay off."

Always the more erudite of the pair, Cube's taking on film like he took on the record industry. Film after film, pleasing the people, and sticking to the well-worn adage of keeping it real, it's all about a masterplan.

"You haven't really seen what's coming with All About The Benjamins and this third Friday," he says. "It's just like introducing Hollywood to a new vision, shit I control. From my mind of one generation to another."

Issue # 69 Fall 2003

CHAPTER 19
TERRORIST THREATS

Somewhere between a 1979 rip off of Grandmaster Caz rhymes over a disco bass-line and the next cash-cow album from Marshall Mathers, some cultural historians are gonna look west for Hip-Hop's first ransom of America's popular imagination. Years after "Rappers Delight" hit radio, you first saw Krush Groove, or the dawn of Simmons even cracked, California kidnapped Hip-Hop from the five boroughs. Don't call the Police: you know it's true. Fly gear gave way to Jheri curl and sweatshirts and the gang-banging matrix that was N.W.A, Dr. Dre and Boyz 'N The Hood transformed American pop consciousness with the gangster and gang culture that every muthafuckin' p.i.m.p. uses to generate record sales today. But according to Ice Cube, Mack 10 and W.C., its all gone wrong.

With the release of Terrorist Threats, the first Westside Connection album since 1996's double-platinum Bow Down, Cube and fam' are looking to hijack Hip-Hop once again. Back in the day, when South Central was looking for the same kind of place on the Rap map that South Bronx had, the target was simple. But today, with east vs west feuds being eulogized on the E! network and financial incentives making regional collabos standard practice, the singles on Terrorist Threats are, like a testament to Cali culture's take on keepin' it real, a call to separate the men from the boys. Jail-time celebrities and wanna-be thugs are targeted on "So Many Rappers In Love". And "Pimp The System" calls out the flesh traders for losing sight of the real whores. Whether they collect on the ransom or not, some of the game's top names are on the list and you can bet a few careers are on amber alert.

Westside Connection - "So Many Rappers In Love"
(https://youtu.be/5H9ASyiIMWw)

Westside Connection - "Pimp the System"
(https://youtu.be/vrC2b9KhCzQ)

This exclusive interview with Ice Cube, W.C. and Mack 10 occurred in a New York City hotel room during the fall of 2003.

Bow Down came out in 1996. Why so long?

Ice Cube: *We always describe ourselves as a family, not a group. There was really no pressure. Timing wasn't right. It was all kinds of things that threw the project off. Time kept extending. The record company was trying to get they shit together in a lot of ways. It just took a minute. With the first album, Bow Down in '96, we felt like the west coast needed a shot in the arm, needed a record to inspire to unify the west coast and shed light on what we was going through in the industry. This time we felt like Hip-Hop is soft, real soft. Without these little beefs that's going on it would be real boring. We felt like that gangster nation really need us. We damn near like the Super Friends. When there's a problem that need taking care of we try to fly to the rescue for the greater good of Hip-Hop. A few reasons why it took so long but that was our focus going in to the project.*

Did you have this album in your heads for a long time? Were you dying to do it?

Ice Cube: *We've been dying to do it for a long time, just circumstances the reason why we didn't do it. When we got in the studios it's like, you know, how you can hold water back and just open it* *up and flood the gates? That's how it was picking up the momentum. We could have did two albums if we had the time.*

I thought you would take this whole concept and your solo career and Westside, bundle it up and sell it to the highest bidder. How did you end up under the Capitol/EMI/Priority umbrella? What do they have on you?

Ice Cube: *They don't have nothing. They just know what they doing right now. They ain't got nothing on us, and they pay. I got a little sour with Priority for a minute, EMI, or whomever you want to call it. I felt like they didn't know what they was doing at a certain time. Now they getting strong again, they really strong out there. We trying to sell records. We have relationships over there, established. I don't want to go to some new record label and I start having to whoop the shit out of some A&R dude. I don't want to do that. I want to be somewhere where they understand that I go make my records and I bring 'em back and turn 'em in; put 'em out. They ain't got shit on me. It's just business.*

Back in the day LL Cool J stepped to Russell Simmons and said, "I need equity. You built your life on my ship". What's going on with you and Bryan Turner? He sold off Priority. Did he break you off anything?

Ice Cube: *(laughs) That's real personal. But I've always been a smart businessman. Let's leave it at that.*

You had Hoobangin', you've had a couple of labels of your own.

Mack 10: *I still got Hoobangin'. Westside Connection on Hoobangin'.*

You put out a stack of records all at once, kept coming, and then it slowed down.

Mack 10: *Really, that's why I did that one record with Cash Money because Priority for a minute was fucked up and everybody was mad at 'em. They didn't know what the fuck they was doing, they was really just fucking people's careers up. You put a record out and they didn't work it, don't promote it, don't do nothing. Some of them records from them young artists I had on Hoobangin', some of 'em were good records and* *they didn't even get a shot at all 'cause they wasn't doing nothing. They had other people on the label that had the attention more than me and Cube done had, even though we was there first. Other people came to the label and the time and attention and focus went right to them, and they was like fuck us. That's really what happened to them records. They was like fuck us.*

Why?

Mack 10: *I don't know. I don't know. We've been around and seen a whole lot of people come and go. A lot of people that they said fuck us for ain't even doing records no more. We still doin' them. But that was in the past anyway, man. We done patched the shit up and we moving forward now. Hopefully they don't make the same mistake again, and if they do we be salty with they ass again.*

From the beginning of time artists have always warned others to watch their business. Why do artists continue to get screwed?

Mack 10: *I don't know, especially nowadays. I really don't have no idea. Everybody know you got to watch your business now.*

Ice Cube: *People are lazy. They don't want to pay attention to detail. They don't want to get into the business part of it until it's too late. Some people want to just rap. People just want to be famous.*

W.C.: *Or just take the quick money.*

Ice Cube: *It's more money than you ever seen in your life anyway, in a while. It's a cheque. Ain't nobody getting no cheques like that. Whether they got money like that it wasn't no cheque. That kind of stuff might start to overwhelm. "Man, they gonna give me $200 000, $300 000 to make a record? Damn! They want to give me that much money to make a record, fine." And they sign and end up owing the record company before the record come out. And they young. The record companies want the young. The old they want to try to phase out 'cause you're too smart for 'em. If you're too smart for 'em, y'all can't do business after a certain point because you ain't that dumb and then* *they feel like they ain't that dumb to give you a better deal, or for you to stay there and just deal you under.*

What happened to Hip-Hop? Why do you think it's so shit?

Ice Cube: *It's a few reasons. One of 'em is the music is soft now. We in a copy cat league. One person start winning off one thing everybody in his same class and under him are gonna try to do the same thing. That's Hip-Hop just went soft. There's too much haterism in Hip-Hop from industry people. They hatin' on motherfuckers who comin' out who been out. They want to throw you away once you been in the game longer than they think you should. They always lookin' for the new booties, so give them three years at being at the top and then start shittin' on 'em too. It's been a cycle that's just been erosion because if the industry is shittin' on the artist, pretty soon the fans are gonna start shittin' on the artist and then everything smell like shit. That's what's happening. There's too much of that. We should understand that your magazines depend on us. We depend on your magazine. It's as simple as that. It's cross collaboration.*

Why is Lennox Lewis gonna fight this bum? Because, the bum got to eat too. He doin' him a favor by fighting him. He givin' him a payday. All this shit work hand in hand, coincide. Now you got rappers against magazines and shit now. You got all kinds of ugly shit in the industry. The music ain't even good no more because nobody says it is. Everybody got a complaint off every album, but it's all money. You want it to be good but you can't really just dis somebody for putting they heart and soul into something. It's venom come out of that.

When you dropped Bow Down you came with a message to get support in the east, it happened, and then the south. Where are we at now?

W.C.: *In '96 we wanted to instill some pride in the west coast and we felt disrespected by some of the outlets and everything, straight up. So we made an album for that time. Right now in the present day Hip-Hop, I think the shit is too soft, we all do, and there's too many motherfuckin' love records on the radio. All the outlets is allowing that* shit to come out and hopefully this album that we did for our fans can reach that other audience. Niggas is tired of that shit. We just trying to bring it back to the essence of Hip-Hop, back to more of the hardcore that was there first. This is the beginning, this is just the first blow. We tired of that shit and that's what we're doing with this album right here. We not just speakin' on that, we speakin' on other issues, as well, but from a gangster perspective. It's a good album, man, and I think that right now Hip-Hop is just too fuckin' soft, too soft. Every record you hear right now, man, is about a female. Every damn record.

Who are the biggest perpetrators?

Ice Cube: *You know. Throw a rock in a pack of dogs and the one that holler is the one that got hit. That's what we doin'. We don't want to point no people out because we ain't even on it like that. We doing this for the greater good of Hip-Hop. We ain't trying to fool nobody. We just trying to change the trajectory a little bit of this, the way shit is spinning. We trying to tip the pass and hopefully intercept it and run it back for a touchdown.*

What happened to the militant Ice Cube?

Ice Cube: *You lookin' at him! You lookin' at him. People always ask me why you don't do records like you did earlier. People got to be receptive to the shit you sayin'. You can't just do the record 'cause you want to do it. That's what happened to Prince - just doing the records he want to do and not feeling the vibe of the people. You got to give them what they want when they want it. You can't just be no fuckin' message man. There's a lot of Emcees careers dead 'cause they was trying to be too political, studious. Time wasn't right. You got to hit the shit when the time is right. Hopefully Terrorist Threats will send a wave through the consciousness of Hip-Hop and the time will be right for another one of them albums like back in the day. I got more shit. I was learning new shit back then, so whenever you want it, man. I'll serve you with it.*

People have labelled you a prophet for what you rapped on before the Rodney King incident and then again with the message Westside Connection predicted, that the music would break over and people would give you love. Why do you three have the vision? How can you see through the bullshit?

Ice Cube: *We ain't from no bullshit, that's how.*

W.C.: *We got enough balls to call it the way we see it. Everybody else see that shit too. They just ain't got balls enough to stand up and speak on it and I think that that's what separates us from the weak. We don't bite our fuckin' tongue.*

Ice Cube: *We don't take no bullshit, don't get no bullshit. Mack, he don't take none, don't get none. You got to come to us straight up, no hidden agendas. Don't put more on it than you telling us 'cause we gonna hold you to it. I think just being them kind of people and being them kind of individuals you sniff out shit faster and being entertainers, where you have people coming at you all the time with bullshit, you become a good detector of it, sniff it out, and we know the game. We know how trends work. We know the cause and effect. We know all that. All that takes place. Like I said, we like the Super Friends. We fly in and do our shit and call us the next time you need us. I think more people will want to put a little more consciousness in the record. This just ain't no dummy album. It's an album that you have to listen to and dissect, but it's street. It's talking to the street. It's not talking to the political climate. It's talkin' to the street, lettin' 'em know about the political climate 'cause a lot of people don't care about reading about that shit. Don't care about looking at the news about that shit. Only way you gonna hear it maybe is in a Rap song.*

What role do women play in your lives?

Mack 10: *Depend on what the woman is. Different women play different roles, depends on who it is.*

W.C.: *Yeah, I feel the same way.*

Ice Cube: *That's a perfect answer. You got all kinds of categories for females. You got babies, you got little girls, you got sisters.*

W.C.: *Mothers.*

Ice Cube: *Mothers, you got.*

W.C.: *Groupies.*

Ice Cube: *Groupies, you got bitches, you got hoes. It's like whatever category you fit into we'll treat you accordingly.*

What's a typical day for W.C.?

W.C.: *Typical day for W.C. is getting up in the morning.*

Ice Cube: *Everybody start with that.*

W.C.: *Yeah, I'm gonna keep it short and to the point. Get up in the morning making sure my business is right. Call who I got to call, make sure my shit is lined up and then getting out and go on the grind. When I say grindin' I'm going out and handling my business, checking my business in the day time, like on the business end whether it's dealing with lawyers or whoever. And night time is studio.*

But you're not a public figure.

W.C.: *Nah, I make appearances. You catch me in the hood, in the streets and shit just hanging out. Going to clubs on the regular I don't fuck around like that.*

Why is Gang-Banger culture such a powerful symbol in America?

Mack 10: *'Cause blood, it's really like that! It's really like that.*

W.C.: *It's a fuckin' way of life, ain't nothin' else but a way of life.*

Ice Cube: *Tribalism is part of the world. It's just another form. It's a vivid, vivid form of tribalism because of the colours. If you ever seen sixty gang-bangers flanked up, with blue on, it's a sight to see. It's a vivid, vivid tribe. The tribalism is on all levels. U.S. Marines is a motherfuckin' tribe. That's why people fascinated with that kind of shit.*

Mack 10: *That's a good answer.*

Ice Cube: *Thank you, 1-0. I appreciate that. That was from top of the dome.*

Mack 10: *Freestyle.*

How has the 'hood you grew up in changed over the past twenty years?

W.C.: *Me and Cube grew in the same neighbourhood, just new faces. I think there's less unity. Money done came in the game and then fucked up the whole car, straight up.*

Ice Cube: *When I was growing up it was a gang of boys on our street of all ages. Our street was full all the time. You would find people playing Basketball down the street, find people in the street over here, find people on the porch down here. Now when I go through there, there's like nobody outside. Everybody just stick to they self.*

W.C.: *It cleared the fuck up.*

Ice Cube: *Everybody cliqued up. It got worse as far as them coming through there killing people. Everybody just to they self, to they family.*

Mack 10: *I think there's more Mexicans. Where I grew up, there's more Hispanics now. The homies is still over there, but like at the High-Schools now, when I was there it was more Blacks going there. Now it's like just damn near even Blacks and Hispanics, or Ese's might have something on us. They might have more over there than we do.*

Where was you head at now to then?

Mack 10: *Then I gave a shit about what was going on in my environment. I can give a fuck less about that shit now, as far as that level. I care about certain people over there and I wish the best for certain people over there. But I ain't fittin' to get get caught up in the hood politics. Like back then I gave a fuck about who was getting along with the neighbourhood and who wasn't getting along with us. It meant something to me. Now, whoever ain't getting along with the neighbourhood, shit, I guess they got to work it out.*

W.C.: *Hell yeah.*

Mack 10: *Don't call me for that.*

W.C.: *We don't give a fuck about a lot of shit that we used to comin'
up in the neighbourhood for the simple fact we done matured a lot now.
It's family first.*

How did Boyz N-The-Hood capture the time and how does it rate
now?

Ice Cube: *It's still one of the classic Black movies that's ever been
made. Back then, what I felt about the movie is that it was a perfect
balance of what we were going through. The gang-banging part of it
could have been just a hair harder, but for the most part it was a great
movie.*

Why didn't you get into clothing lines like everyone else?

Ice Cube: *They're trying to make money. Me, myself, I just don't
want to wear myself too thin. I'm looking at the bigger picture. I'm
looking at doing something for a minute changing into shit I'm sixty,
seventy years old. I don't want to do that. I don't want to just pimp
everything I've got to give. Not yet, I might need to do a clothing line
someday for real. I don't want to do it 'cause I can. I'll do it when I
should do it or when I need to do it.*

What else do you have to say?

Ice Cube: *Tell everybody to buy Terrorist Threats. Do yourself a
favour. It's a masterpiece. I think the more you listen to it the more you
like it. It's every song is a good one, from singles to the in-betweens.*

What do you need people to know about?

Mack 10: *That Westside Connection's album will be out December
9th. That's really it. I don't really care about nothing else at this point,
just Westside Connection. When it comes to business, that's all I really
give a damn about, for real.*

Tour?

Mack 10: Got to tour. Gonna spot date until the end of January, February. We'll be on the road getting it.

What do you have coming up?

Ice Cube: We shootin' a few movies called Are We There Yet?, a movie called Willy.

W.C.: *Starring W.C.*

Ice Cube: And a movie called XXX. I'm gonna be working in-between. I'll be promoting this record, touring.

photo by Patrick Nichols
LAUGH NOW, CRY LATER August 19, 2006 Toronto, Canada

CHAPTER 20
ICE CUBE TALKS LAKERS & RAIDERS

t's no secret that the west coast's most prolific lyricist and Hip-Hop's head honcho in Hollywood is also a Lakers and Raiders lifer. For Ice Cube, it's all game related. This is an exclusive summer 2006 interview with Ice Cube that occurred in a Toronto hotel room.

What's your favourite Raiders team?

Ice Cube: 1983 team. Won the Super Bowl. You got Plunkett... Wait a minute... I might want to take that back because that '80 team was the shit too. They didn't have Marcus Allen, but they had Plunkett and Cliff Branch, Ty Christensen, Rob Martin. Had some good players. Ted Hendricks, Art Shell, Gene Upshaw.

And now? Sapp, Moss, Aaron Brooks.

Ice Cube: I think they trying to get it together, but I don't know if that's the squad. I'm just not a big fan of Aaron Brooks. He seems like a player that got all the skills but just don't have the desire to be the best. The game seem like it comes easy to him. He's out there kinda getting his money. I don't see no fire in him. You don't know if he threw a touchdown pass or an interception when he walks to the sideline. It's the same expression.

Kind of the poor man's Michael Vick?

Ice Cube: In a way. I just think he's like Lamar Odom in cleats. He can ball. He got the skills. But do he got the desire to be the best? He got all the tools he need. On that level you gotta bring it. You can't get up there nonchalant. I think his game is nonchalant. I think he drops back too slow. I think he releases too slow. I think his ball comes out slow. To me that's a nonchalant attitude because Peyton Manning's ball don't come out slow. His shit come out quick! Fire on it! I think it's just the approach to the game.

How do you think Larry Johnson is going to do this year?

Ice Cube: He got a new Coach and new Offensive Coordinator. I don't know how he going to do because you change those two pieces; Herm Edwards is a defensive cat. When I saw their two pre-season games it looked like they were going backwards, which I'm real happy about that because you talking 'bout the Chiefs, right? I don't care if they win a game. I want them to lose every game, fire all the Coaches and waive all the players. I'll be a happy man. They in the same division as the Raiders and I don't want them, San Diego or Denver to win shit.

Any thoughts on the NFL draft?

Ice Cube: Houston is stupid as hell. That's got to be one of the dumbest things I've ever seen. But hey, whatever. No reason in the world they shouldn't have took Vince Young. The Quarterback they have sucks. He's weak and they done put a gang of money behind him. They should have took Vince Young, even if the team sucked. He's so loved in Dallas that they stadium would have been filled. I think that's a franchise player. Defensive Lineman, unless you got Reggie White, is not a franchise player. Them dudes, I ain't going to say they come a dime a dozen, but it's not hard to find somebody for defensive line. To me, you go with your franchise players. The first guy that got picked? What's his name? (Mario Williams) All I know is Reggie Bush and Vince Young. I think when you get a draft pick you get the cream of the crop because you can always move people.

Any predictions on Super Bowl 2007?

Ice Cube: Football is a hard thing to predict because you don't really know what teams look like until that eighth game when you know who's good and who's not. I'm sitting here saying I don't know because it's some good moves during off season. Every team looks good. Even the super-strong teams have lost pieces. Pittsburgh and Seattle done lost some intricate pieces. Pittsburgh lost the "Bus" and they don't have Randle El no more. And Seattle lost, I think, Hutchinson, who's a beast, and kept Sean Alexander running. So no telling what they gone look like.

Switch it up to Basketball. The all-time greatest Lakers team?

Ice Cube: Wow! Of course Magic, Kareem, Byron Scott, James Worthy and Michael Cooper. I think it was about '87-'88.

So Showtime kills Shaq, Kobe and all that?

Ice Cube: Oh yeah, all day, because Showtime was running. It was the unit playing as one. With the Shaq era it's a forced unity because of the triangle offense, so it's not really everyone playing as one. It's scripted passes and scripted cuts. It's unfortunate. It's a great team, but not as great as the 80s.

Your all-time team has Shaq and Kobe on the bench?

Ice Cube: All-time? If I ever put an all-time team together? Kobe's not on the bench. I think Byron Scott is on the bench. Go with Magic, Kobe and I'd still put Kareem in the middle. Shaq might look crazy as a Power Forward and have Worthy as a Small Forward.

Could Kobe play with all those guys?

Ice Cube: Yeah. People think that Kobe is a selfish player. Being better than everybody, it's just hard to respect their game. He's just better than everybody on the Lakers, for a long time. The Lakers, especially Shaq and Kobe, just got off on the wrong foot. Kobe was a rookie and Shaq was a vet. They probably didn't think that Kobe was going to make the team because he was a short High-Schooler and there weren't any in the league, so they probably treated the boy bad. He was from Europe and he just wasn't going for that. He's a different kind of cat. He ain't from here, in a way. He didn't appreciate it, so when he became a man he was going to give a little back. That's what I think really happened.

So off court behavior doesn't have anything to do with it? Ratting out Shaq?

Ice Cube: I don't believe he ratted out Shaq. Shaq never said he ratted him out and Kobe never said he ratted him out. The only person that said he did it was the Police and the media. Who's going to believe them? I never heard Shaq say he ratted him out. I never heard Kobe admit that he said nothing. Once they knew the case was going to get dropped this whole little interview pops out. I don't believe he said that stuff.

Are you a Lakers season ticket holder?

Ice Cube: Yep. It was good the first three years I had it and I don't know what the hell happened from then. I had it ever since they won they first championship. I got a box at the Staple Centre. But it's been mighty dry since then.

Do you go to every game you're in the city for?

Ice Cube: Mostly. If it's a Friday night, crazy traffic and they just playing the Bobcats then I might watch on TV. All the other ones I'm there. My son is a fanatic. Six years old and he's a fanatic.

Were you at the infamous 81 point performance against Toronto?

Ice Cube: Hell no, man! Hell no! I wasn't' there. I was in Mexico. I got a phone call from my older son saying Kobe's going crazy. He was at the game. He says 'Kobe is going crazy!' I say, 'What you mean?' He say, 'It's like he glowing! He got 69 points! It's the 3rd quarter!' I was like, 'What!?' 'He got 69 points, it's the third quarter, five minutes left to go. This is crazy.' Looked at the news at the end of it and he got 81. I missed it, but I got it on tape!

Did Steve Nash deserve the double MVP?

Ice Cube: *When I first heard they was going to give it to him I was like, 'Man, he don't deserve it.' But then just watching him play, dissect the Lakers in so many different ways, I was like, 'The dude is bad!' For a Point Guard to be that unstoppable; stop the pass, shoot, stop the shot and pass. It's nothing you can do with it. He got the energy and he can get the ball in the hole in every angle, any angle. When dude's scoring 35 points and still dishing out 12 assists, you're a bad boy. I want Kobe to get it. I think the league don't want Kobe to have it. I don't know how you can have a player like that and not get the MVP with all the years he played. Last year I thought he was going to be able to get it by having great games. I almost want him to get that more than the championship.*

What does it say about a guy who was born in South Africa, grew up in British Columbia and turned out to be the two-time MVP?

Ice Cube: *It don't say nothing. He good enough to be in the league. It's not where you're from, it's where you're at. If you're good enough to be in the league, you're worthy of the MVP. The league is a standard in Basketball and if you can make that standard I don't care where you come from, you should get the respect of the pro players.*

What are the Lakers chances this season?

Ice Cube: *Go to the playoffs, they got a good chance. Anything past that, no chance. They don't have enough big players in the paint. Until that happens you ain't got no chance to win a championship.*

Who's going to take the NBA Finals this season?

Ice Cube: *I don't know who could beat Miami, man. I thought Dallas had 'em but they couldn't finish it. I just don't know who else is that strong. I don't even know if the Suns or Amare Stoudemire could even do it. That'll be their first time on that level in a long time, so it'll be Miami.*

CHAPTER 21
ALBUM DISCOGRAPHY

N.W.A

N.W.A and the Posse - November 6, 1987 (Macola Records)

Straight Outta Compton - August 9, 1988 (Ruthless Records/Priority Records)

100 Miles and Runnin' - August 14, 1990 (Ruthless Records/Priority Records)

Efil4zaggin - May 28, 1991 (Ruthless Records/Priority Records)

Ice Cube

AmeriKKKa's Most Wanted - May 16, 1990 (Priority Records)

Kill at Will - December 18, 1990 (Priority Records)

Death Certificate - October 29, 1991 (Priority Records)

The Predator - November 17, 1992 (Priority Records)

Lethal Injection - December 7, 1993 (Priority Records)

Bootlegs & B-Sides - November 22, 1994 (Priority Records)

War & Peace Vol. 1 (The War Disc) - November 17, 1998 (Priority Records)

War & Peace Vol. 2 (The Peace Disc) - March 21, 2000 (Priority Records)

Laugh Now, Cry Later - June 6, 2006 (Lench Mob Records)

I Am The West - September 28, 2010 (Lench Mob Records)

MC Ren

Kizz My Black Azz - June 30, 1992 (Ruthless Records/Priority Records)

Shock of the Hour - November 16, 1993 (Ruthless Records/Relativity Records)

The Villain In Black - April 9, 1996 (Ruthless Records/Relativity Records)

Ruthless For Life - June 30, 1998 (Ruthless Records/Epic Records)

Reincarnated - October 31, 2009 (Villain Records)

Dr. Dre

The Chronic - December 15, 1992 (Death Row Records/Priority Records)

Dr. Dre Presents... The Aftermath - November 26, 1996 (Aftermath Entertainment/Interscope Records)

2001 - November 16, 1999 (Aftermath Entertainment/Interscope Records)

Compton - August 7, 2015 (Aftermath Entertainment/Interscope Records)

Yella

One Mo Nigga ta Go - March 26, 1996 (Scotti Bros. Records)

Westside Connection

Bow Down - October 22, 1996 (Priority Records)

Terrorist Threats - December 9, 2003 (Priority Records)

CHAPTER 22
WHO IS HARRIS ROSEN?

They call me Heller. For thirty years my life was a blur of hyper-focused activity. One moment I was living in my parents suburban Toronto basement and the next in the midst of a whirlwind of multiple musical cultural revolutions that occurred throughout the 90's and 2000's.

I fell in love with music at an early age and attended my first concert, Hall & Oates, at the age of thirteen. I turned to Metal and Punk and travelled to Montreal to attend festivals and once ended up in a crash pad sharing the floor with the Cro-Mags. I discovered the Beastie Boys Rock Hard EP and RUN-D.M.C. King of Rock album, dove into Hip-Hop and then dug beneath the surface and became wrapped up in the Jazz sounds of John Coltrane, Miles Davis, Thelonius Monk, Art Pepper and Eric Dolphy. I read Beneath The Underdog: His World as Composed by Mingus and then picked up out of print paperback copies of Black Music and Blues People by LeRoi Jones. By the time I graduated Hip-Hop had taken over.

As an avid music fan and vinyl enthusiast I applied for and was awarded an afternoon slot on community radio station CHRY 105.5 based out of York University. Though it was short-lived when I put a friend's phone call live on air and he made an unacceptable comment. I attended College where I became Manager of the in-house closed circuit radio station and contributed to the campus newspaper. One of my first interviews was with DJ Jazzy Jeff & The Fresh Prince. I went to shows at the local Masonic Temple, also known as the Concert Hall, and witnessed legendary artists such as Public Enemy and Big Daddy Kane, and traveled to the mecca New York City and bought "12 vinyl like Kool G. Rap and DJ Polo's "Poison" in the heart of Times Square.

In 1988 N.W.A's Straight Outta Compton and Ice-T's Power were released and I became an ardent fan of west coast artists and what has been labelled gangster rap, reading books by Iceberg Slim and Donald Goines to further comprehend the street life detailed in their raps. I attended the 1990 New Music Seminar in New York City and witnessed Tupac Shakur perform with Digital Underground on a bill with De La Soul and Live Squad, and was in the host Marriott Marquis Hotel when Ice Cube and his former Ruthless Records label-mates Above The Law infamously staged a "battle royal". During this trip I also came to face Ice Cube who signed a copy of his classic AmeriKKKa's Most Wanted. In the fall of 1991 I witnessed the Toronto debut of Cypress Hill that led to the creation of "Insane In The Brain". Chubb Rock had shared the bill with them and became enraged when the Promoter directed him to take the stage before Cypress Hill. Listen to the cadence of B-Real's vocals on the chorus.

Peace! Magazine was conceived in the winter of 1991 by Raymond Wallace and Ken Lock, who worked at the Scarborough Town Centre HMV in the east end of Toronto. The store was a lightning rod for Hip-Hop. In the fall of that year, a Naughty by Nature autograph session had erupted into an infamous mall riot. I joined the team, Raymond Wallace and I each anted up $3500.00 and together we released the debut issue in March 1992. It was sixteen pages on newsprint and featured exclusive interviews with Dave Grohl of Nirvana, Geto Boys, Beastie Boys and Bjork's group, The Sugarcubes.

Peace! was my third stab at the magazine game.

In 1989 I co-founded a Heavy Metal magazine with a megalomaniac who was known to cross dress. Let's call him Gepetto. The platform was built to promote a glam rock band he managed at the time named Succsexx. The magazine was called M.E.A.T., an acronym for Metal Events Around Toronto, and we operated out of his two bedroom apartment on the subway line and an after-hours production hub downtown inside a law office adjacent the Eaton Centre.

It was an exciting time in music. The new breed were beginning to break down longstanding barriers and had begun to land on radio, tv and magazines with an unseen fervor. Sadly, Gepetto was caught up in his own archaic world, the significance of the new music revolution went straight over his head, we no longer saw eye to eye and parted ways. Grunge and Punk movements usurped Heavy Metal. Gepetto politicked and plotted with the major labels, donned a Cowboy hat, posed beside Garth Brooks and published a short-lived Country magazine. Years later it was revealed the downtown production office we had used was responsible for millions in illegal immigration scams culminated by the suicide of a disbarred lawyer.

Magazine stab number two The Cutting Edge formed in fall 1991. I partnered with Joey Vendetta, who was acting Music Director at Canada's leading Rock Radio station Q107 and instrumental in breaking artists and bands nationally. Good times while it lasted, however we parted ways after a year due to a creative difference. Dropping Hip-Hop content into The Cutting Edge was a no go with Joey. A few years later he moved south of the border to the U.S where he worked on the other side of the table for a few labels. Joey is currently Senior Vice President Strategic Marketing Partnerships and Publicity for Live Nation Inc., based in their Beverly Hills corporate office.

Hip-Hop had become an unstoppable force in my life and there was no stopping it. I was not the only one taking in multiple genres of music. There was an undeniable void in the market, especially in Canada. When Peace! Magazine began, it filled a void here in Canada. Other than a short interview on the national music television station, MuchMusic, or an ultra-rare extended look on the weekly The New Music, options to discover and learn about upcoming artists was virtually nonexistent. Mainstream media rarely, if ever, took advantage of the opportunity to speak with the artists in this series.

In its early stages, Peace! Magazine was a music publication that mashed up Hip-Hop, R&B, what was known as Alternative at the time, and a cross section of the electronic music revolution from Techno and House, to Euro Pop and Drum N' Bass. Over time it evolved into a lifestyle publication with fashion, athletics, gaming, sneakers, travel, film and more while picking up national distribution in three chains, on the newsstands and key independent locations across the country.

The music was selling everywhere. This was the age of multi-platinum albums and compilations. Key releases shipped by the tens of thousands and sometimes gold and platinum as marketing budgets increased exponentially. Artists were frequently flown to Toronto for promotional duties and when they were too active back home the labels flew us direct to them for an exclusive.

Engrossed in most of the music that we covered, I approached interviews with a desire to ask and learn what I personally wanted to know, challenging artists to dig deep into themselves for responses. No question was out of line, if presented in the proper light and there was no reason to ask what I already knew, or to reproduce the promotional biography and its tales for the benefit of the labels.

Life at Peace! was a whirlwind of activity. As a hands on Publisher I enacted almost every element necessary on the back end too. Including communication with staff, publicists, marketing departments, advertising agencies, printer, shipping and delivery components. I attended trade shows, expos and conferences all over the world traveling to six continents and was there either in person or on the phone and compiled a true and honest archive of audio, images and video.

Independent publishing demanded a superior level of hyper-focus and I had it in abundance. Unfortunately I had exhibited multiple characteristics of A.D.H.D. (Attention Deficit Hyperactivity Disorder) my entire life and brought stress and drama to many people around me and myself throughout the years. Following the birth of my son Louis I was professionally diagnosed, medicated, and completed an MCBT (Mindfulness Based Cognitive Behaviour Therapy) program. I strongly recommend Success Through Stillness: Meditation Made Simple by Russell Simmons & Chris Morrow to anyone who is interested in improving their life.

Setting the tone from the first issue, Peace! featured non-stop exclusive interviews with a veritable directory of artists, designers, executives and athletes who changed the world and lorded over pop culture at one time or another, many of whom perpetually continue to endure at the top and you will read about in upcoming volumes of the series. To name check a select few; Dr. Dre, Daft Punk, George Clinton, Sean Combs, Beastie Boys, Eminem, Destiny's Child; and sadly many who are no longer amongst us but left behind a rich legacy such as Notorious B.I.G., Kurt Cobain, Malcolm McLaren and Aaliyah.

The journey of creating In Their Own Words: Behind the Music Tales of Truth, Fiction & Desire began in September 2014. I uncovered and pored over hundreds of cassette and micro-cassette tapes and thousands of print photographs digging deep into my personal archives. The ability to draw from the original audio recordings is crucial and truly sets this series apart. A 1997 conversation I had with Muggs in Los Angeles has always stuck in my mind. We met to discuss his upcoming solo debut, Muggs Presents The Soul Assassins, Chapter 1. One month later I returned for an interview with Mr. Scarface. I called Muggs and he read the cover feature in front of me and said, "You actually wrote what I said", and thanked me. I was taken aback; Until that day I'd assumed that every interview I read was a true representation of what the artists stated. I was naive. During the run of the magazine various artists would tell me they were often misquoted by the press with facts twisted in order to fit a format or portray them in a negative light.

Much of what you will read, see and hear here has been sensationalized by others in a manner of journalistic psycho-speak. The typical approach is mapped out as a Masters thesis, pulling media quotes and lyrics, paraphrasing and analyzing the artists thoughts years after the exact creative period. A few may even offer a new interview with the artist, who will reflect back on a time in life with what we hope is 20/20 vision, though it's not a guarantee. In the words of Johnny Rotten, 'Boring, Sidney. Boring.'

In Their Own Words: Behind the Music Tales of Truth, Fiction & Desire is a series that captures the mood and the feel of the energy that surged through music in the 90s. Live and direct from the exact cultural forces who carved it out, in their own words and voice. This is their story to tell.

This series is as close to the truth as one can get. It delivers raw thoughts by real people and is manifested directly in the voice and words of the artists who made it happen. This is their story to tell, with context, images, curated quotes, behind-the-scenes reports, anecdotes and colour.

In Their Own Words: Behind the Music Tales of Truth, Fiction & Desire is a continuing series. I strongly suggest you sign up for the mailing list to receive updates on upcoming new releases, free books and much more.

Harris Rosen, July 2015.

Twitter: @MrHeller1
Facebook: https://www.facebook.com/NWAbook &
https://www.facebook.com/peacemagazine/
http://behindthemusictales.com/series-books/

REVIEW REQUEST

If you enjoyed this book kindly post an honest review. Your support matters and it really does make a difference. I do read all the reviews so I can get your feedback and I've made a number of changes to this current edition as a result of that feedback.

If you would like to leave a review then all you need to do is go to the review section on the book's page where you purchased it. You will see where to do it – click and you are good to go.

Thank you for the support.

Harris

FINAL REMINDER

This is your last chance to grab your free copy of:
New York State of Mind (Part 1)

To receive your free copy of New York State of Mind (Part 1) with vintage exclusive 1992 and 1993 interviews with Intelligent Hoodlum/Tragedy Khadafi, Pete Rock & C.L. Smooth, Leaders of the New School and Brand Nubian – Soldiers sign up to our mailing list with your first name and email at behindthemusictales.com

The In Their Own Words: Behind the Music Tales of Truth, Fiction & Desire series has allowed me to share my extensive archive of exclusive interviews with you in much greater depth.

Some of the upcoming series you will hear exclusive audio and see exclusive photos are:

The Real Eminem: Broke City Trash Rapper

Daft Punk: Behind the Robots

Destiny's Child: The Writing's On The Wall

Beyonce, Kim, LeToya and LaTavia

New York State of Mind (Part 1)

Intelligent Hoodlum, Brand Nubian, Pete Rock & C.L. Smooth, Leaders of the New School

New York State of Mind (Part 2)

Afrika Bambaataa, Sean Combs, DMX, Funkmaster Flex

Magnolia: Home of tha Soldiers

Behind the Scenes with the Hot Boys & Cash Money Millionaires

Lil Wayne, Juvenile, B.G., Turk, Mannie Fresh, Birdman and Godfather Slim

pr-EDM (Part 1)

Kevin Saunderson, Moby, Malcolm McLaren and Todd Terry

The Grunge Years: 1989 - 1991

Nirvana, Pearl Jam, Alice In Chains, Soundgarden and Courtney Love

Legends of Hip-Hop (Part 1)

RUN-DMC, Beastie Boys, GangStarr and Nas

Ice-T, Bodycount & the Home Invasion of America

The Evolution of Funk, Rhythm & Soul (Part 1)

George Clinton, Bobby Brown, TLC and Erykah Badu

Deep Inside the Real Mary J. Blige

The Metal Years

Metallica, Megadeth, Slayer, Exodus, Iron Maiden, White Zombie

Rock N' Roll Legends (Part 1)

Kiss, The Replacements, The Black Crowes, Red Hot Chili Peppers

Reggae Nights

King Jammy, Buju Banton, Sizzla, Snow

California Love (Part 1)

Boo-Yaa T.R.I.B.E, Del Tha Funky Homesapien, Coolie and MC Eiht

The MAGIC of Fashion: Las Vegas Revisited

Marc Ecko, Russell Simmons, Karl Kani and Carl Jones

To receive your free copy of **New York State of Mind (Part 1)** sign up to our mailing list with your first name and email at behindthemusictales.com

I am only looking for your first name and email. Once you are set up on the list you will receive periodic emails with a link to the next In Their Own Words: Behind the Music Tales of Truth, Fiction & Desire Sampler. You can opt out at any time.

Made in the USA
Lexington, KY
02 November 2017